TWAYNE'S WORLD AUTHORS SERIES

A Survey of the World's Literature

SPAIN

Janet W. Diaz, Texas Tech University.
Gerald E. Wade

EDITORS

The Spanish Picaresque Novel

TWAS 557

THE SPANISH PICARESQUE NOVEL

By PETER N. DUNN

Wesleyan University

TWAYNE PUBLISHERS
A DIVISION OF G. K. HALL & CO., BOSTON

Published in 1979 by Twayne Publishers,
A Division of G. K. Hall & Co.
All Rights Reserved

Printed on permanent/durable acid-free paper and bound
in the United States of America

First Printing

Library of Congress Cataloging in Publication Data
Dunn, Peter N
The Spanish picaresque novel.

(Twayne's world authors series ; TWAS 557 : Spain)
Bibliography: p. 155–62
Includes index.
1.   Spanish fiction—Classical period, 1500–1700—
History and criticism.   2.   Picaresque literature—History and criticism.
I.   Title
PQ6147.P5D8   863'.03   79-1030
ISBN 0-8057-6399-6

Contents

About the Author

Peter N. Dunn has been Professor of Romance Languages and Literatures at Wesleyan University, Middletown, Connecticut, since 1977. Born in England, he completed his studies at the University of London and taught for sixteen years at the University of Aberdeen, Scotland. In 1964–65, he was Visiting Professor of Romance Languages at Western Reserve University, Cleveland, and from 1966 until 1977 was Professor of Spanish Literature at the University of Rochester.

His previous books are *Castillo Solórzano and the Decline of the Spanish Novel* (1952), an edition of Calderón's *El alcalde de Zalamea* (1966), and *Fernando de Rojas*, also in TWAS (1975). He has also published many articles and book reviews on Spanish literature, ranging from medieval poetry and prose through Cervantes, the seventeenth-century drama, and other topics. He has lectured in the United States and abroad.

Preface

This book concerns a number of prose fictions written in Spain in the late sixteenth century and the first half of the seventeenth, which have come to be called collectively "the picaresque novel." I have tried to examine each one as fully as space allowed, and also to show how each one reveals both its dependence on and its emancipation from its predecessors. As we read we discover that there is no simple and clear process of evolution but rather that the earliest novels remain the most influential. These early novels—*Lazarillo de Tormes, Guzmán de Alfarache, Pablos the Cheat (El Buscón),* as well as Cervantes' contributions—are the great innovators, and *great* is the word which should be stressed here because the later writers all strive after novelty. For these reasons the books treated here are not apportioned equal space. Some are simply better and more interesting than others by any standard, though I hope to have dealt fairly by all. I will go no further in anticipating the conclusions of this study, because it is a fair assumption that the reader of it is also a reader of novels, and a work of literary history should, like any other work of fiction, aim to sustain curiosity and, if possible, to delight with surprise.

Some readers will be disappointed to find nothing here about picaresque literature in English, French, or German, which followed on the translations from Spanish into those languages, or on the recrudescence in our time of a mode of writing commonly called picaresque. That would have required a different book from the one that I was asked to write. Defoe, Smollett, Fielding, Scarron, Le-Sage, Grimmelshausen are all important in their own right, and I am not sure that anything valuable would have been achieved by giving them a few lines apiece at the end of a book on Spanish novels. It would rather have imposed a distorted perspective, and my hope is that readers who do know the works in these other literatures will at least get to know the Spanish a little better and can then make their own comparisons. Included in the bibliography are some works which do discuss picaresque in a wider European context, and particular attention is drawn to them.

As is usual in this series, all quotations are given in English, and the versions are my own. Most of the novels which have been translated were done very freely or are not in current English, which does not suit our limited purpose.

Page references are made to the anthology *La novela picaresca española*, edited by Angel Valbuena Prat (2d ed. [Madrid: Aguilar, 1946]) This is a convenient collection, but some of the texts in it are less reliable, and in these cases the following editions are referred to: *La novela picaresca española*, edited by Francisco Rico (vol. 1, 2d ed. [Barcelona: Planeta, 1970]) (for *Lazarillo de Tormes*; Alemán, *Guzmán de Alfarache*); Quevedo, *La vida del Buscón llamado don Pablos*, edited by Fernando Lázaro Carreter (Salamanca: C.S.I.C., 1965).

The following are not in the Valbuena collection: Gregorio González, *El guitón Honofre*, edited by Hazel G. Carrasco. [Estudios de *Hispanófila*, no. 25 (Chapel Hill, 1973)]; Anonymous, *Segunda parte del Lazarillo de Tormes* (1555) (in *Biblioteca de Autores Españoles*, vol. 3); Juan Cortés de Tolosa, *Lazarillo de Manzanares*, edited by Giuseppe Sansone. (Barcelona: Selecciones bibliográficas, 1960). Other good modern editions are listed in the bibliography.

My special thanks are due to Wesleyan University, Middletown, Connecticut for the generous grant of leave and research funds which enabled me to finish this book, and to my wife for her critical vigilance in reading it.

Chronology

CHAPTER 1

Picaresque, Pícaro

I The Word pícaro

IN English, the word "picaresque" is simply an adaptation of the
Spanish *picaresco*, and the *Oxford English Dictionary* attests its
earliest use in 1819, though the noun "picaroon" had been current
since the early seventeenth century. Its reference is almost exclusively literary. If we refer to so-and-so as a picaresque character, or
to a picaresque situation, we count upon our listeners' being able to
evoke, however vaguely, the qualities of a literary type, much as we
do when we call an event "melodramatic" or "farcical." There is no
convenient substitute. When Frank Wadleigh Chandler wrote his
influential book on picaresque literature in 1899, and sought,
perhaps, for a term more accessible to his readers, he titled it *Romances of Roguery*. "Rogue," "roguery," "knave," "knavery," have
been used, but are now faded and old-fashioned. How would we
refer to Guzmán de Alfarache or Pablos if we were to meet them in
present-day style and surroundings? They were part adventurer,
part tramp, part jack-of-all-trades, part confidence trickster. Their
very versatility makes it impossible for us to find one word to fit
them in their various guises and at the diverse stages of their careers.
Because although we may speak of a picaresque incident, what we
are accustomed to look for in these novels is the shape of a whole
career, an attitude to life, beyond the novelty of the separate incidents and the variety of occupations.

Much less has been written since the closing years of the
nineteenth century about the origin of the word *pícaro* and its shifts
in meaning. Its earliest recorded occurrence appears to have been
in a morality play by Bartolomé Palau *Farsa llamada Custodia del
hombre* (after 1541) in augmentative form *picarote*, and in a context
which suggests a wrongdoer or maker of mischief. In 1548 and again

11

in 1560 Eugenio de Salazar uses the word *pícaro*, the first time opposing picaros to courtiers, and the second time putting picaros among thieves, swindlers, gamblers, counterfeiters, vagrants, and other undesirables. At this stage it is difficult to decipher exactly what specific meaning is to be ascribed to the word, or indeed whether there is a specific meaning within the general sense of someone who does not settle down in one place and who lives by his wits as circumstances allow. This was the way Alfonso de Pimental used the word ca. 1590, and perhaps it represents well enough the usage of the day.[1]

Pícaro does not occur in *Lazarillo de Tormes*. This may be because the word was too slangy at that time, or because its everyday sense could not embrace the roles and the aspiration of the protagonist. But it is used by Alemán of his creature Guzmán, who then becomes *the* picaro for seventeenth-century readers. Somehow a word and a book have come to depend on each other. Whether or not the everyday use of the word has become more current and the social type to which it refers more frequent and clearly recognizable is not easy to say, but we may notice an important difference between *Lazarillo de Tormes* and *Guzmán de Alfarache* which probably has a bearing on the matter: Lázaro would not use the word of himself because he desires to be seen by others as, first a victim of ill luck and second, as one who has achieved a position of respectability. Guzmán, on the other hand, is writing what is from one point of view a confessional tract, so that he will be the first to call himself a rogue and a cheat. From this point on, *pícaro* is inseparable from literature. If the proliferation of vagabonds and small-time adventurers gives to the literature a topical reference, the novels (and other literary evocations, in drama, narrative poetry, and satire) modified the readers' perceptions of the picaro as a social and moral phenomenon.

The term *pícaro de cocina* ("scullion," "kitchen boy") is found in 1611 (not in 1525 as has been claimed)[2] and it is used in such a way as to suggest a boy who did the most menial jobs and lived off the scraps. It may not have referred to his role in the kitchen so much as to the fact that those who were recruited mostly were picaros from the street and that in order to survive they would still have to support themselves as sharp-witted rascals.

The etymology of the word has given rise to lengthy argument, and to some wild speculations that we can ignore.[3] From *pícaro* is derived the adjectival form *picaresco*. But there is a noun *picardía* which means "the actions, or way of life, of a picaro." The presence of the *d* in *picardía* suggests Picardy (the region of Northern France) as its origin. Since the final *d* (or *t*) in the adjectival *picard* was not pronounced, this could account for the difference between the noun and the adjective in Spanish. Furthermore, the accentual shift in Spanish, *picáro > pícaro* has parallels in other nationality names: *Bulgaria/búlgaro; Hungría/húngaro; Tartaria/tártaro*. It would have been helped by the vogue for proparoxytones at the end of the century, and by support from the verb *picar* ("prick," "mince," "itch," "sting"). Picardy was a part of France which Spaniards knew better than most in the sixteenth century, by trade (especially by reason of the manufacturing and textile towns of Lille, Cambrai, Contray) and by war (Picardy adjoined the Spanish Netherlands which were in revolt during much of this period). Picardy (Picardía) then became synonymous with a land teeming with refugees, vagrants, deserting soldiery who looted and pillaged, all of them living by their wits off the land and never being allowed to settle in one place. Moreover, a returned Spanish soldier, writing of the events of 1577–92, mentions the Flemish and Walloon boys who carried the Spanish soldiers' knapsacks, and we recall Cervantes' boys Rincón and Cortado whose entry into the picaresque life was as porters in the streets and markets of Seville.

II *The Setting*

The series of novels called picaresque extends from 1554 to 1646, from the last years of the reign of Charles V to the middle years of that of Philip IV. Charles V (Charles I of Spain), Holy Roman Emperor since his election in 1519, had attempted to heal the ideological breach in the Christian church. He first sought to favor such moderate intellectuals as Erasmus in their desire for reform, and to avoid a showdown with Luther, in the hope of effecting a reconciliation. Later, when he saw that conciliation was no longer possible, he resorted to warfare backed by political alliances. In earlier years he had also hoped to carry the crusading fervor across the sea into Africa with his assaults on Algiers and Tunis, and in the spirit of old-fashioned chivalry he had once offered to fight Francis I, king of France, in single combat. He enjoyed reading the novels of chivalry parodied in Cervantes' novel *Don Quixote*. And Cervantes was a contemporary of Alemán, whose eponymous Guzmán de Alfarache inhabited a world as far distant from the polite fictions of chivalry as could be imagined. During the reign of Charles (1516–56), Spain's empire grew to an undreamed-of size and wealth, but Europe's religious unity under Rome was lost forever. Even the sweetness of that power and wealth turned sour as the gold bullion from the American continent was pledged to German bankers in order to pay for Charles' military campaigns against Protestants, Turks, and French, his diplomatic missions, his German court. Dreams of world leadership were buried with Charles when he retired to a monastery and abdicated in favor of his son Philip, in 1555–56, though there were still advisers, preachers, and orators who would urge Philip II to pursue that aim in years ahead.

As Spain's empire and influence grew, so did the fear and rivalry inspired by her power, and thus opposing alliances were founded on that fear and that rivalry. France and Spain were at war on and off for most of the hundred and fifty years from 1500 to 1650. Both France and England found allies of convenience in the Protestant Netherlands, which carried on a war of independence against Spain's overlordship during the reigns of Philip II and Philip III.

A middle-aged reader of *Lazarillo de Tormes* would have heard his father talk about the days when Castile, Aragon, Navarre, and Portugal were separate, independent states. In fact, Spain was only united territorially as late as 1492 when the armies of Ferdinand and Isabel took Granada from the Moors. From 1580, after the death of the childless king of Portugal, Spain had not only joined Castile and its American possessions to Aragon with its Mediterranean territories in Italy, Sicily, and Sardinia, but the Portuguese empire in Brazil and in Africa and the Far East, from which the spice and slave trades could be dominated. This was the empire upon which, it was said, the sun never set.

There is no great empire, however, without inner stresses, no world ambition without insecurity. Grandiose dreams hide mediocrity, injustice, and suffering. These are not new lessons, but each generation and each rising nation has to discover them for itself. And the most potent means of self-discovery, and of exploring the inner contradictions of a culture, is in the arts. This is what makes the appearance of *Guzmán de Alfarache* and the first part of *Don Quixote*, within a few years of each other, so significant and fascinating a coincidence. Each of them burrows, from its own starting-point, and with its own preferred technique and perspective, into the painful areas of self-delusion and empty dreams.

Here are some bare historical facts. The reign of Philip II was a succession of financial crises and crashes; increasing taxation fell heavily on the common people, and those who were able bought titles of nobility, thus avoiding taxes. The taxes raised continued to be pledged in advance to foreign bankers. Moreover, the union of the crowns of Castile, Aragon, and Portugal had not resulted in a unified administration, unified taxation, or a uniform judiciary. There was enough centralization to provoke regional resentments, but not enough to override them. The weaknesses could not be hidden in the years 1639–40, when Portugal seceded, Catalonia declared itself subject to France (with which Spain was at war), and Andalusia also attempted to gain independence. The plagues and famines of 1600–1605, the flight of landless peasants into the cities, the expulsion of the Moriscos (1609–14), the denial of advancement to Christians of Jewish ancestry (the so-called "conversos")—all were factors which increased social strains during the period when the picaresque novels were being written.

The rapid growth of Seville as a large cosmopolitan center (the only one in Spain to surpass 100,000 inhabitants by 1600) with industry, international trade, banking, and commerce, is undoubtedly related to its attractiveness to picaros who were seeking both opportunities and anonymity. It has often been said that the picaresque is a literature whose protagonists are motivated by hunger, and that for this reason Seville and Madrid, with their poverty, their beggary, and their crime, became favorite locations for these novels. However, it should be remembered that almost all the novels after *Lazarillo de Tormes* show the picaros, male and female, making and often losing large sums of money. The principal cities were centers of great wealth as well as of poverty, and the kind of audience implied by the novels of Salas Barbadillo and Castillo Solórzano was most likely the nouveaux riches who were joining the urban aristocracy throughout this period, and who desired to be seen at the extravagant entertainments ordered by Philip III and Philip IV. The rural areas, which suffered the enclosure of common lands, the evictions of small farmers and tenants early in the 1600s, plus the natural disasters of plague, famine, floods, and crop failures, were felt to offer less hope, which explains why people continued to flow into the towns and cities. If the writers of picaresque novels had been concerned only with the fact of hunger, they would not have chosen an urban setting for most of the events.

This period was one of exceptional activity in all of Europe; of discoveries in optics, astronomy, mechanics, pure mathematics, and anatomy; of new philosophical speculations; and of new intellectual models of justice and society. During this period a Spanish Jesuit, Juan de Mariana, would produce arguments and conditions to justify regicide (his work was burned in Paris), and Spain produced a series of ecclesiastical lawyers who would continually raise the question of the legitimacy of making war upon Indians, of expropriating their territory, and of enslaving them. It is a time of new literary and artistic experiments in all forms. The Spanish picaresque novel does not reflect scientific discoveries, or new speculations about the nature of the physical world, just as it does not reflect society in a precisely literal, realistic way. Rather, one might say that it is itself a discovery, a new means for extending human consciousness of the existential process of a human life, captured from within, in contrast to the incidents and adventures seen from without.

CHAPTER 2

Lazarillo de Tormes *and its Continuations*

*T*HE *Life of Lazarillo de Tormes, with his Fortunes and Misfortunes,* usually known simply as *Lazarillo de Tormes,* was published in 1554 in three separate editions, the two which are most alike appearing in Burgos and Antwerp (the Low Countries, or modern Holland and Belgium, being Spanish possessions at that time). The third, longer version, was printed in the university town of Alcalá de Henares. We do not know who the author was nor when the book was written, and cannot say with certainty which of the three editions is the earliest, or what is the relation between them. There may be a lost edition (or editions) of 1553 or earlier, from which our surviving texts derive, or perhaps all three were cashing in on the success of a work which had been circulating in manuscript. A number of likely explanations have been offered. The novel was reissued in 1573 with some cuts which had been ordered by the censor of the Inquisition. It achieved an enormous popularity in the next century when booksellers had it reprinted so as to capitalize on the success of *Guzmán de Alfarache.*

The date of composition cannot be discovered either from external or from internal evidence. Mentions of Charles V's campaign, and a session of Cortes, could allude to two different pairs of dates: 1510 and 1525, or 1520 and 1530. We are reading a work of fiction, which means that the historical allusions are included for their appropriateness to the story. Moreover, a lapse of fictional time must be supposed between the last events that are narrated and the narrator's setting down his story in writing. Another historical allusion, which may be accurate, is Lázaro's reference to famine and the consequent decrees against beggars and tramps entering the city of Toledo. This, it has been suggested, would fit the lean years of the 1540s. Thus, there seems to be no reason to depart from the com-

17

monsense assumption that the book was written shortly before the first printing, in other words, in 1552–53.

The identity of the author, like the dates of composition and first publication, has been hidden from us. Various candidates have been put forward, and the two whose claims appear to be strongest are Fray Juan de Ortega, who became general of the Hieronymite order in 1552, and Diego Hurtado de Mendoza, a poet, diplomat, and historian. Neither of them is inherently improbable, and both fit Claudio Guillén's observation that the author "must have been an independent, critical spirit."[1]

Outwardly, *Lazarillo de Tormes* consists of a prologue and seven chapters (called *tratados*) of unequal length: the first three taken together provide about four fifths of the whole. As a story, it is a partial autobiography which begins with the narrator's birth and his few recollections of childhood, proceeds through the hardships of his service with various masters, and ends with his satisfaction at having achieved a position of relative comfort, security, and self-esteem. It is a model of concision, and of ironic understatement, which makes it all but impossible to summarize.

I *The Plot*

In the first chapter Lazarillo is born not beside, but *in* the river Tormes, from which he takes his name as a literary figure. His father was a miller, and the mill where the mother gave birth was set within the stream, as was usual. This tells us immediately that the book is antichivalric, for it rejects all those grand sounding names like Amadis de Gaula, Lisuarte de Grecia, and the grand adventures they undertake. The father was convicted of stealing flour from his customers and died in an attack on the coast of North Africa. His mother left the mill for the city where she took in washing and served a commander. At this time she took up with a Negro stablehand and presented Lazarillo with a dark-skinned little brother. When a blind beggar asks to have Lázaro for a guide, the mother agrees, gives the boy some standard advice to be good, and sends him on his way. His education in life now begins. The blind man (all the characters henceforth are nameless) is tightfisted and cunning. He knows every penny of the earnings from alms and from the reciting of prayers, every crumb of his meager food, every drop of wine. The boy is hard put to survive, and does so only by engaging in a relentless battle of wits, in which he takes some beatings. For example, he drinks from his master's wine jar by means of a straw, and the blind man brings the jar crashing down on the boy's face. Finally, he runs away, and joins a new master, a priest, who is even more miserly than the blind man, but with less excuse. Moreover, he is hypocritical, giving callers the impression that the boy has a free run of the pantry. The priest himself lives well, mostly in other people's houses, and Lazarillo has to develop subtle ways of stealing from the bread box, which is always kept locked, and around which silent battles of cunning and deceit are continually being joined. Being an acolyte as well as house servant, he eats his fill only when his master is called to a wedding or a funeral; so he prays that others may die in order that he may live. He stays with this terrible priest because he fears that a third master might be even worse, though he cannot conceive how that could be so. But his master throws him out of the house after discovering that he is the "snake" which has been getting into the bread box; Lazarillo has a duplicate key, which he keeps hidden in his mouth while he sleeps; unfortunately for him, his breath hisses through it, the priest believes he has found the snake and, in the darkness, brings a heavy stick down upon the boy's head.

The third master is more promising: a squire (an *escudero;* that is, an *hidalgo* of the lowest rank). But a long walk through the streets of Toledo from morning until mid-afternoon followed by their arrival at a gloomy and almost bare house undeceives Lázaro. His master, he now realizes, walked past the food stalls not because his house was well-stocked, but because he has no money. He has nothing but his aristocratic pretension, his concern for appearances, and a nobleman's loathing for menial work. Lázaro now has to fend for both of them, which he does by begging and by attracting the sympathy of neighbours. The squire disappears at the end of the month, without paying the rent, leaving the boy to face the creditors. The next sections are all much shorter. Chapter 4 has only a few lines on his service with a friar, but they are full of innuendo. Chapter 5 shows him accompanying a pardoner who fakes miracles in order to bring in money. The next chapter is one of the shortest—only a few lines longer than chapter 4—but it covers the longest span of time, for, besides serving a painter who decorates tambourines, he spends four years as a water-carrier, paying rental to a chaplain who owns the donkey and the route. The final chapter shows him established in public office as a town crier; behind this official facade he is also to be found taking his cut from the sale of wines and other things, and married to a woman who is publicly reputed to be the mistress of the archpriest, his patron.

II   The Materials of Narrative

The story of *Lazarillo*, then, is a memoir, an account of the narrator's life from his birth until some time before the moment when he chooses to begin writing. This is characteristic of the major novels which follow *Lazarillo* (Alemán's *Guzmán de Alfarache,* Quevedo's *Life of Pablos the Cheat,* Alcalá Yáñez's *Alonso, Servant of Many Masters*), though other novels in the seventeenth century are told differently. The whole is ostensibly written for an unknown person whom Lázaro addresses as "Your Honor" ("Vuestra Merced") during his narration. The prologue tells us that this person has requested, or commanded, an explanation of an undisclosed "matter" (*el caso*), and so Lázaro complies by telling his life story. We shall return later to the question of the motivation of the novel. It will be clear that we have to distinguish three levels of consciousness in the narrator: that of the boy whose past is being relived (no doubt, selectively) as it is related; that of the mature man who finally reached the "peak of good fortune"; and that of the narrator who organizes the story and puts his life into words. It will be convenient to denominate these three levels with different names. Since Lazarillo is a diminutive form of Lázaro, we shall use that name to designate the boy, up to the end of his emergence as an adult in chapter 6. The name Lázaro will be reserved exclusively for the man in his final situation, with career and family. Lázaro as writer will be referred to as "narrator," unless the name Lázaro seems more desirable in order to avoid awkwardness.

Let us begin the analysis by recognizing that many of the incidents are not original, but belong to previous literature or to oral tradition, in the form of jokes and stock situations.[2] There are scattered bits of evidence in plays and in drawings, for example, which suggest that the pair "blind man with guide boy" had become a commonplace. A fourteenth-century manuscript in the British Library shows just such a pair among its marginal illustrations. There the boy can be seen practising various deceptions on his master, such as stealing a chicken, slitting his sack, and drinking from his jug of wine with a straw. The blind man and his boy appear as the subject of farces in medieval France, and even the name Lazarillo is found attached to a figure who does outrageous acts with a naivety which may be either natural or assumed. Many of the separate incidents can be found elsewhere. The blind man's trick of leading Lazarillo to a stone bull, telling him to put his ear close to it and listen, and then giving him a blow on the head; Lazarillo's trick of making his master take a running leap at a stone post, on the pretext that he needs to jump over a flooded gutter; his stealing his master's sausage from the fire and replacing it by a hard turnip, all of which occur in the first chapter, are examples of stories and jests which appear to have been traditional. Possible literary origins have also been suggested for the pardoner's false miracle, in chapter 4. The squire may also be seen as conforming to a stereotype, namely, the impoverished *hidalgo*, as vain as he is hungry, and obsessed with his honor. Verbal caricatures of his type proliferate in the sixteenth and seventeenth centuries, in novels, on the stage, and in satirical verse.

These anecdotes and incidents, as well as others which have not been mentioned, belong in the main to a tradition of popular comedy, and it must be remembered that *Lazarillo de Tormes* is indeed a funny book. Changes of taste during intervening centuries may have made us less inclined to laugh at crashing blows on the face; laugher in such circumstances was probably a means of warding off the insistent brutality of a great part of everyday life. On the other hand, we still laugh when clowns knock each other down or have doors pushed in their faces, and there may be something for us to learn in this fact. Readers were not always as serious about literature as we have become. It is not that the craft of writing was not taken seriously, or that poems and stories could not be read as model situations, but rather that literature had not come to command the sustained emotional sympathy which readers have commonly extended to fictional characters in the last century and a half.

There are, of course, many funny incidents which do not contain physical violence. Lazarillo's repeated penetration of the priest's bread box, first as a mouse, then as a snake, boring new holes as fast as the priest can cover the old ones, resembles the dizzy chases in the silent film comedies. There are various levels and styles of comedy, too, from the verbal quips to the ambivalent wordplay which reveals duplicity of mind, and from acts of ingenuity in the struggle for survival to the absurd discrepancies between intentions and the means available to fulfill them. When we recognize this, of course, we are also acknowledging that the book is something more than a collection of amusing incidents kept together by one person's narrative, more than the sum of its parts collected from oral tradition and previous literature. What is interesting and original in *Lazarillo de Tormes* is the way that the fragments, which have no artistic significance in themselves—indeed, they might appear to resist artistic development—are organized into a narrative, made to belong in a life which is in process. None of the later picaresque novels has this characteristic, and the point is worth stressing.

III   *The Blind Man*

These jokes and tricks serve to advance the narrative in *Lazarillo*, to transform the character or the situation. For example, the incidents mentioned above and which occur in chapter 1 in connection with the blind man are linked in more than one way, both with the development of Lazarillo's career and among themselves. The first, that of the stone bull and the blow on the head, is followed by the old man's comment, and Lázaro's reflection:

"Stupid! That'll teach you that a blind man's boy needs to know a trick more than the Devil," and he laughed a lot at the joke. I felt as if I awoke right then from my innocence, like a child that's been asleep. I said to myself, "What he says is true; I must keep my eyes open and look sharp because I'm on my own, and must think how to get ahead."

This incident sets the keynote for the boy's dealings with his first master. Also, by extension, it defines his goal in life: survival first of all, and then a pure pragmatism in "getting ahead." At the end of this chapter when he has made the old man run his head against the post, Lazarillo abandons him. Thus there is a symmetry to the chapter, since it begins and ends with similar acts of violence, but there is also a progression, for the victim of the first act has become the victor in the second. If the first marks the point zero of innocent simplicity, the second measures the advance which has been made. Lazarillo has indeed learned one trick more than the Devil, and has played it and won. In addition to serving as a frame within which the episodes of Lazarillo's life with the blind man take place, these two collisions also have an organic relation to what is placed between them. When Lazarillo finally runs away, leaving his master stretched out on the ground, he taunts him triumphantly by referring to the previous episode of the sausage and the turnip, "How did you smell the sausage, but not the post? Olé, olé!" (27). Thus, in addition to being an act of revenge which is suitable to the beginning, the end is the triumphant culmination of the arduous struggle which has been taking place. This struggle has taken place on more than one level. In the first place, Lazarillo has battled with his master in order to increase his miserable ration of food, in order not to starve. Secondly, there is in much of Lazarillo's activity a pursuit of ingenuity, a wit expressed in action. This of course is what makes Lazarillo's tricks amusing for the reader, rather than just crudely practical. Survival can become a game, an art, to the extent that the means used for survival exceed the material goal and become gratuitous play. Thirdly, the struggle between the boy and his master is not merely the local one between this boy and this man, but is a fragment of the universal and ambivalent struggle between those who have power and those who are dominated, between age and youth, between father and child. The struggle is ambivalent because it contains the desire to turn these power relationships upside down and, in turning them upside down, to start the game over again. Finally, the signal that the relationship is at an end is not any rite of passage based on acceptance or harmony, but a violent separation which nevertheless reveals that the pupil has learned all that the master had to teach him.

Thus Lázaro assimilates his first model. We have seen just a few of the ways in which the first chapter of the story holds together in form and in meaning, although it is built up out of apparently diverse ancedotes from folk tradition. However, it not only has unity within itself, but contributes to the whole by setting up some signs which will not acquire their full value until later. So in the incident of the wine jar, the blind man bathes the boy's wounds with wine, and comments, "What do you know, Lázaro? The same thing that laid you low is bringing you back to health" (20). Again, after the affair of the sausage, as the wily old man is treating the boy's wounds with wine, he observes,

"I tell you that if any man in this world is going to be fortunate with wine, it's you."
The people who were washing me really laughed at this, though I'm damned if I found it funny. But the blind man's forecast was not wrong and I've often thought of him since then and how he must have had the gift of prophecy. And I've been sorry for the bad times I gave him, though you could say I've paid for them seeing that what he said that day turned out later to be so true, as your honor will hear. (25)

We, like Lázaro, are unable to see the full import of these words until we reach the end of his narrative, that is to say, the stage of his life at which the blind man's words can be reflected upon and seen to be prophetic. He will indeed owe his "good fortune" to wine (the archpriest's) in the final chapter, and in that sense the prophecy is a device for aligning the beginning of Lázaro's career with its end. The effect of this is not merely to give a mechanical unity to the narrative but to convey, by means of this unity, the continuity of consciousness in the narrator. We are not permitted to forget that it is Lázaro *the man* who is writing, though something of the boy has survived in the man. When we come to the end and look at the shoddy accommodations he has made, his pride in his ignoble profession, his hypocritical assertion of his wife's virtue, the cynicism of the conclusion will be impossible to miss. At the same time, we may reasonably guess that Lázaro's cynicism, like that of any real person, is not all cheerfulness underneath, and there are moments when the text represents the various superimposed layers of his consciousness, as it does in the passage just quoted. Beneath the smugness we glimpse his fear that later events have really been a punishment for the times when he took advantage of the blind man.

IV   *The Priest*

The second chapter, in which Lazarillo is servant to a miserly priest, is organized differently. The blind man shared the little food that he had, and taught him cunning. He announced at the outset, "Gold and silver I cannot give you, but advice on how to live, that I can teach" (14). He learns to meet deceit with deceit, to avenge himself, to swallow his humiliation until he can take revenge, and he observes his master's command of counterfeit piety. The blind man's double role of provider and mentor which is implied in the relationship of substitute parent is certainly degraded, but it exists and is recognizable. In the priest this is no longer the case. Also, the blind man embodies an ancient literary motif: namely, the association of physical blindness with keen insight. This is familiar to us in such figures as Teiresias the blind prophet in *Oedipus Rex*, Homer the reputedly blind poet, and in the linking of Gloster with Lear in *King Lear*. The opposite is the case with the priest, who starves the boy from the first day without ever suspecting, apparently, that he might be the cause of the bread disappearing. He suspects mice at first and then, after boarding up the box, he is baffled until his neighbor suggests that there is a snake in his house. In each case, the wrong explanation allows Lazarillo to adjust his mode of stealing so as to conform to what is expected of a mouse or a snake. If the priest does not suspect the boy during all this time, the explanation cannot be that he is too charitable. It must be that he is too egotistical and too stupid to know that the boy is starving, and to see that he has a motive for taking bread. To see that would be to see himself as the cause of the boy's hunger. It is made clear that the priest who, by his vocation, should be both provider and mentor, is neither; he who should be alert to the needs of his neighbor, sees nothing. He is purely negative, a void, and this gives us the clue to the proliferation of religious vocabulary in the mouth of Lazarillo during this chapter, and his apparently blasphemous reverence for the bread as the "face of God" upon opening the box (33). If the duties of a Christian mean nothing to the priest, how should Lazarillo know any better? If the person whose profession calls him to imitate Christ can live without reverence, and if God and Christ are empty words, how should Lazarillo fill the void except with what he most desires and needs in order to stay alive? The fact that bread is a religious symbol anyway, and that the consecrated bread is the body of Christ, makes Lazarillo's ecstasies over it reinforce the harshness of the satirical portrait of the priest. That is to say that the satire is anticlerical, rather than anti-Catholic. The person in this novel who supposedly lives by Christ does nothing to mediate Christ to his servant boy, and consequently the words "God," "Christ," and so on, become synonymous with material food, or with social success. The priest is finally responsible for this desacralizing of the world as it appears to Lazarillo.

V *The Squire*

The next master is the squire, and this chapter is in some ways the most complex of them all. Again, the relationship of the boy to his master is different from formerly, the tempo is different, and so are the internal proportions of incident, dialogue, and comment. To begin with, Lazarillo appears to have found a master of superior status, to judge by his bearing and his dress, but time disenchants him. Appearance and time both assume enormous importance in this section and are closely woven into the structure. From the moment that the squire engages Lazarillo, he spends the rest of the morning walking about the city of Toledo in the usual aristocratic exercise of letting himself be seen. Clocks chime, bells toll, the hours pass, and there is no sign of preparations for a meal. The master gives no orders to Lazarillo to purchase anything in the market, and when they enter the house, it is silent and deserted. Master and boy dissemble to each other; the former says that he ate breakfast and will need no more until night; the latter replies that he is no great eater and has a reputation for frugality. The true situation is dramatically revealed when Lazarillo produces his crusts of bread and goes aside to eat them, and is followed by his master with ravenous curiosity. So they share what the boy had begged, and from now on he supports his master, too.

The first hours are filled with that mutual dissembling. Lazarillo was impressed by his new master and he wishes to impress, in return. So, when he is asked about himself he relates, "I gave an account of myself lying as best I could, telling the good things and keeping the rest quiet . . . " (44). When it has become clear that there will be no food that day: "Sir, I'm a boy who doesn't worry too much about eating, thank God. I can say this for myself, that among all my friends I'm the smallest eater, and I've been commended for it by all my masters up until now" (45). When the squire brings a jar of water Lazarillo, thinking it is wine, interjects in order to give an impression of temperance, "Sir, I don't drink wine" (46). Finally, that same night, he assures the squire, "For my part, Sir, you don't need to worry; I can spend a night, or even longer if necessary, without eating" (47).

The squire and the boy grow closer on the basis of their common hunger and their common hypocrisy. When the master opens his mind to the boy, he tells how he finds it impossible to go into service because all levels of nobility above himself are insufferable, demanding and giving nothing in return. His ideal would be to wait upon a grandee,

"If I could find such a one I would make a great confidential secretary, and I'd satisfy him a thousand ways. I could lie to him as well as the next man and butter him up no end. I'd laugh at all his jokes and mannerisms, even if they weren't the best in the world; I'd never say anything to annoy him even if it were in his interest, and I'd always be very attentive in word and action. I wouldn't go out of my way to do things well unless he were likely to see them. I'd tell the servants off where he could hear me, to give the impression that I was really concerned about him. . . ." (62–63)

This is the man who tells Lazarillo (59–61) that he left his home town in order not to have to raise his hat to another man (an acute point of honor) and who, at the end of the month, decamps when the rent-collector appears.

As Américo Castro has observed, the squire is the only one of his masters with whom Lazarillo carries on a dialogue.[3] Many readers have felt the current of sympathy that flows between them, as nowhere else in the book. Lazarillo realizes that the squire is really penniless, not just niggardly like his previous masters (54). But these observations need to be supplemented before we draw conclusions from them. It is true that whereas the boy is tricked and shoved by the blind man, starved and ignored by the priest, he is talked to—or rather, talked at—by the squire. The talk, however, is not only an occasion for human warmth, but rather for self-justification, an art which Lázaro will use—is using, in fact, in his own narration as we read it. The two speakers exchange advertisements for themselves. Lazarillo ingratiates himself, and the squire asserts his honor, his concern for "what they will say." Each on his own side creates an appearance: the squire presents his to the world and incidentally to Lazarillo, while the latter presents his to the squire and incidentally rehearses the skill in outfacing the world which he will fully employ in chapter 7. The boy also discovers from the man how selectively the concept "honor" may be employed. For example, the squire asks Lazarillo whether the bread which he is eating was "kneaded with clean hands" (i.e., with pure-blooded Castilian hands). The boy is unable to give an answer, so the master relishes it anyway. Thus the conversations are part of Lazarillo's apprenticeship in manipulating appearances. While he builds his own facade he continually pierces his master's by sustaining a subversive counterpoint of muttered comments under his breath.

Chapters 4–6 are very different from the preceding ones. They present a period of years in a few short pages. The fourth master, a friar of the Order of Mercy, leads a life the character of which is indicated by insinuation: "He hated singing in the choir and eating in the monastery, couldn't resist going out, loved worldly affairs and visits, so that I reckon he wore out more shoes than all the rest of his community together" (66). After a very short time, Lazarillo leaves him because of the fast pace, and also because of things he would rather not mention (67). The next chapter is taken up almost entirely with the pardoner's false miracles by which he conned the faithful, and chapter 6 sets him up as a water-carrier, in which situation he is able to save money and buy his first suit of respectable clothes. Lázaro is no longer the same little boy as at the beginning, but is taking his own place in the world. This is finally achieved in chapter 7, with the special "arrangement" between his wife, the Archpriest, and himself, that we mentioned earlier.

VI The World of Values

One might characterize *Lazarillo de Tormes* as a *Bildungsroman*, that is, a novel which traces the growth and formation of the mind and personality of the chief character. When he leaves home, his mother tells him, "Try to be good, and God be your guide. I brought you up, and I've found you a good master. Now you're on your own" (13). The following chapters show not only some of the events which take place in the company of his various masters, but how he is influenced by them. On the other hand, there is no introspection in this novel, Lazarillo does not pause to analyze his progress at stages in his personal development. The novel does not follow any ideological assumption about a preferred system of pedagogy, about educating the emotions and the reason, etc.; nor does it go to the opposite extreme of representing a life which develops in response to the absolute randomness of experience. At this level of organization, the book has a sequence which is ironic rather than exemplary. Values are neither asserted nor called into question; rather, assumed traditional values are pictured in a state of dereliction, each man embodying the value opposite to what he normally represents (probity, charity, honor, etc.) in his social being. As a result, Lazarillo becomes an appropriate product of that sequence of negative models.

In this sequence we should include the boy's parents: his father a thief, his mother the mistress of a stablehand. None of these adults is a great criminal or impressively evil. On the contrary, they are all models of small-scale sordidness. After his parents, the adults to whom he owes most are the first three masters. In fact, Lazarillo says himself of the blind man that "after God, he gave me life, and although he was blind he lighted the way and led me on the road of life" (14). The cunning that he learns during this period is attested to by the priest when he dismisses Lazarillo with the words: "It's impossible that you can have been anything but a blind man's boy" (41). It is in these first three chapters that Lazarillo's experiences are presented in greatest detail, and as part of a cumulative process. As these experiences are absorbed and internalized, so he becomes adapted to the world.

From this point of view it is interesting that the first three masters represent, respectively, the three estates of medieval society—commoners, clergy, nobility—each of them at the lowest and poorest level.[4] Whereas the acquisitiveness of merchants and bankers, the scheming *Realpolitik* of prelates, the vanity and arrogance of the high nobility might be dazzling enough to achieve grandeur, there can be nothing impressive about the representatives of social vices when they are reduced to this level of pettiness. I do not mean to suggest that the author's purpose was a comprehensive social satire. Rather, we might say that the existence of a powerful tradition of social satire enabled the unknown author to present, with great economy, a world in which the strongest impulses are nowhere ethical or altruistic. Experience in such a world, without guidance, will produce an individual who is a cynical reflection of that world, and that is what Lázaro has become by the time he recounts his life.

At this point we might notice the name Lázaro (Lazarus), with its two familiar biblical examples. The one (Luke 16:19–23) concerns the beggar Lazarus who lay in his wretchedness at the gate of Dives, the rich man. As Lazarillo becomes Lázaro and grows in prosperity, he too becomes complacent, like Dives. The other is the Lazarus who was raised from the dead (John 11:1, 17, 38–44). There are a number of references to death and resurrection in *Lazarillo de Tormes*, notably the tomblike house of the squire which terrifies the boy; the three days he was unconscious after being beaten by the priest, which he likens to the three days spent by Jonah in the belly of the whale (traditionally presented as prefiguring Christ's three days in the tomb). The significance of this may be summed up briefly in the words of A. D. Deyermond: "we see a character who turns from Lazarus into Dives, and who is apparently raised from worldly death to wordly life, but is in reality plunged from moral life into moral death. The two aspects of Lazarus point in the same direction."[5]

VII *The Shape of a Life*

We observed earlier that the words of the blind man on the importance of wine in Lázaro's life are prophetic. Prophecy is just one literary technique among others for linking distant points in a narrative, or for making the end justify the beginning, and we can find some of them here. The first is that the situation in which Lázaro sees himself at the end is not very different from that of his parents when he was a child. The irony of the structure is apparent: it is ironic because it means one thing to the narrator but another to the reader. The narrator sees his success; he has arrived at the peak of his good fortune, having broken out of the rut and made his own way. The reader sees his ignominy; by a circuitous path he has come to a point where he reenacts his own beginnings. There are verbal ironies also. A mother might express the hope that her son will be as good as his father, even perhaps that he will be better. Lazarillo's mother trusts in God that he will "turn out to be no worse than" his father (13). When the mother moved away from the mill after losing her husband she did so with the intention of "getting in with respectable people, so as to become one of them" (10), and when Lázaro responds in chapter 7 to the archpriest's urging to think of his advantage and not listen to gossip about his wife, it is by means of the same phrase: "Sir," I said, "I made up my mind to get in with respectable folk . . ." (79). The irony is stronger in the Spanish, because the word for the respectable folk *(los buenos)* really means "good people," so that the discrepancy between goodness and respectability, between what the words say and what they mean is stated with an Ibsen-like ruthlessness. Near the beginning, the narrator identified virtue with rising in the world and vice with sinking. One might suppose that in his career, if in nothing else, Lázaro has escaped the model of his parents, but once again he is mocked. His father was punished and exiled for his thefts, his stepfather and his mother were flogged as a punishment for their irregular lives, and the former was greased with hot lard as well. The "peak" of Lázaro's good fortune is to occupy the post of town crier, which is a public office, and which ought then to confer prestige. But just as Lazarillo, when he was a boy, served masters who were the lowest members of their respective classes, so now he is the lowest kind of public official. He is lower even than the public executioner, whom he would serve as assistant. Part of his duties would consist precisely in proclaiming the sentences meted out to offenders such as his parents, exposing them to public shame. And the position (the "royal appointment," as Lázaro proudly calls it [77]) far from being an honorable one, conferred infamy on the holder, who was disqualified from pursuing a respectable career, in the army, for example.[6]

Lázaro's life, up until the point at which he begins to narrate it, has followed a double trajectory. First, a rise in material well-being. But this has been achieved as the result of the lessons in astuteness, amoral pragmatism, and hypocrisy that he has learned in the company of the first three masters. So we observe that the material rise is accompanied by a moral descent, a decline from innocence to sophistication, in the proper sense of this much-abused word. The double movement is not simple and direct, because it is complicated during the first three chapters by the presence of hunger as the prime motive for action, and by a parallel series of other contrary movements. For example, the boy's fight against hunger does not diminish, but increases as his masters rise in social standing. Again, at the moment when his material situation is worst (i.e., when he is having to support his master as well as himself) we see him engaged in the only acts of generosity which figure in his career. It is obvious that we must be careful in speaking of the "hunger-motive" as a necessary characteristic of picaresque fiction. It undoubtedly plays a larger part in *Lazarillo* than in any of the later novels, yet we can see already that there is a hunger for security, for a comfortable position (even when this has to be maintained by cynically suppressing the inherent contradictions) which is at least equal to the hunger for sustenance. One may "survive" in one sense of the word while destroying oneself or being destroyed in other senses, and the unknown author has played these senses brilliantly one against another.

It is natural for readers to feel sympathy for a boy who is pushed out of his home and apprenticed to a grim series of masters, by whom he is starved and roughly treated. If the reader is not alert to the internalizing of experience, to Lazarillo's assimilation of his models, it may come as a shock to see him in his final posture as the contented cuckold, glorying in his illusory respectability, proud of his ignominious profession. But the author has provided additional assistance to the reader in chapters 4–6. There, the masters are mentioned much more cursorily, the content is no longer the sufferings and anguish of Lazarillo seen close up, and time is no longer experienced as the passage from one wretched or brutal incident to the next. Now we are given anecdotes in which the feelings of Lázaro are not presented. Years pass in a few lines (chapter 6), so that when we once more gain a closer view of him, in the final chapter, we are reintroduced after a lapse of time during which it is to be assumed that his personality has become definite and he is a responsible adult who no longer needs to plead hardship for stealing. But we are given some clues. At the end of chapter 6 he buys his first suit of clothes. They are secondhand, he is stepping into other men's clothing. He also dons a secondhand sword, and as he does so he finds that his trade of water-carrier is not compatible with his respectable appearance. His idea of respectability is firmly linked to "what they say" and "what they think of me." Then, at the beginning of chapter 7, he briefly joins a constable as assistant, but runs away at the first occasion of danger, leaving his master to face the assailants and get badly beaten. We are reminded of the squire who ran away and left the boy alone to face the creditors. Once again, the antichivalric tone is clear.

It should be clear by now that *Lazarillo de Tormes* is a complex little work, containing multiple symmetries and multiple ironies.[7] Within the period of Lazarillo's service with the blind man there are strict symmetries, and the episode ends with the boy's revenge for the blow he suffered at the beginning. The formative masters form a set of three, and the book itself has three phases in its development corresponding to boyhood, emergence from dependence, and final status as a man.[8] These symmetries would have little meaning on their own if they did not point up the ironies, the moral symmetries. The ménage à trois of the end has its precedent at the beginning. The physical dependence of Lazarillo on his first three masters is reversed at the end; his freedom symbolized in buying clothes and sword introduces his moral and social dependence on others. Not only his clothes are secondhand; his wife is too. So is his facile view of respectability which consists of keeping up appearances and swearing loud but empty oaths upon his wife's virtue. Hunger for bread gives place to hunger for acceptance. The prophetic phrases of the blind man, the various foreshadowings which we have observed, also make for a tight unity. But the foreshadowings would scarcely be possible or effective were it not for an aspect of the work which we have taken for granted until now, and which is fundamental to the formation of the picaresque novel. I refer to the fact that it is written as autobiography.

The novelty of the unknown author in creating the autobiography of a character who commands no admiration, enjoys no social preeminence, and has no profound thoughts to deliver, was absolute.[9] There were memoirs, literary epistles, and novels written through the viewpoint of a first-person eyewitness, but *Lazarillo de Tormes* imposes upon the reader a completely different orientation from any of those. The important matter, anyway, is not what kinds of precedent may or may not have been combined in the mind of an unknown author, but what is achieved by his innovation. As Lázaro is telling his story, we are not reading purely and simply about his childhood, but the way the man Lázaro sees his childhood, or rather, the way he wants the reader to see it. Then again, he is writing to command, that is, the reader for whom he writes is not you or me but that "Your Honor" whom he addresses from time to time. So we may suppose that he is telling his story in such a way that "Your Honor" will be impressed, or at any rate satisfied. Can we be sure, then, that Lázaro is giving an honest account? Or is he putting a fairer face on things? Is he telling his story in such a way that we will be induced to think his shoddy life is all the fault of his parents and his harsh childhood? Who is "Your Honor," and what is the "matter" that he wants Lázaro to clear up? Is it, as has been suggested and as most critics now take it, the irregular marital arrangements of Lázaro that excite "Your Honor's" interest?[10] But why should a personage of "Your Honor's" standing be concerned about the sordid marriage of an executioner's assistant, who is presumed to be without honor in any case? Considering that the archpriest who is Lázaro's patron is also "Your Honor's" "servant and friend," perhaps he is more concerned for the reputation of the cleric than that of the town crier.[11] But why does he approach the "matter" by way of Lázaro? Is he a person of some power and authority, the bishop or his representative who is making tactful inquiries before making an accusation? Or is he a prying busybody? A voyeur? Or, since nothing is inconceivable in Lázaro's world, is he a more influential priest who would like to dislodge the incumbent and take over the archpriest's mistress?

If we don't know who "Your Honor" is or the motive for his requesting an explanation, it is difficult to assess accurately the tone of Lázaro's reply. Is the final chapter cynical self-display masquerading as frankness, or is it genuine frankness in reply to an investigator? Or is it Lázaro's way of saying "This is my nice little setup; if you want to take over from the archpriest, this is how high you'll have to bid"? The questions grow broader as one proceeds from the picture of Lázaro's "domestic bliss" in the final chapter to the narrative as a whole. Why, in answer to a question about the "matter," does Lázaro decide to tell his life story? Is it in order to excite pity? To offer his past hardships as an excuse for what he is now? Is he saying, "Look, I've come a long way by my own effort; it's been a rough life and now that I've made it, don't you rock my boat"?

Although we may not be able to answer these questions unambiguously, what is clear is that we, placed by the narrator in the position of "Your Honor" reading Lázaro's reply, must not be deceived by his self-righteousness. Early in chapter 1 the narrator refers to his little half-brother who ran away from his black father crying "Mamma, bogeyman!" This prompts the reflection, "How many people there must be in the world who run away from others because they can't see themselves!" (11). Some commentators have been prepared to take this phrase to heart, and to see in it evidence that the book bounces its moral criticism back at the reader. "If we turn aside in revulsion from the man that Lázaro has become, are we not closing our eyes to potential or actual corruption in ourselves?" asks A. D. Deyermond.[12] I have never heard of anyone turning aside in revulsion from Lazarillo; it is certain that many people have laughed, and one should not ignore the therapeutic and antiseptic value of laugher. Indeed, nothing would be more likely to make Lázaro laugh up his sleeve than to know that his life story had made "Your Honor" beat his breast and confess that he is no better, because then the narrator would have succeeded in his tactic of making humanity to blame. After all, it was Christ and not the adulteress who said "He that is without sin among you, let him first cast a stone at her" (John 8:7). It makes a great difference who says it.

To conclude, *Lazarillo de Tormes* creates a new literary form, the fictional autobiography of a shabby opportunist of disreputable origins. The unknown author has used materials from folk tale, but the way they are put together is not that of an entertainer who simply uses them in sequence. They are, surprisingly, made part of an individual's experience, they enter his memory, and they shape his future responses. As Fernando Lázaro Carreter has expressed it, "*Lazarillo* emerges from an aggregate of folk stories which condition its structure. . . . But . . . it is also true that the author frequently strives to elude this conditioning, to break out of the folk mold in

search of a new architecture" (63–64). The possibilities opened up
by the first-person narrative, by the deviousness of the narrator, and
by his self-justification through writing, will be taken up by later
writers, though not immediately. Too much in *Lazarillo* was new for
it to be imitable, as we can see by briefly studying the attempted
continuations.

VIII   *The First Continuation*

The anonymous *Second Part of Lazarillo de Tormes* was published
in Antwerp in 1555. In it Lázaro joins the army to fight in North
Africa, and is shipwrecked near Algiers. Having filled himself with
wine, he is saved from drowning because there is no remaining space
in his body for the seawater to enter. He fights off some tuna fish
with his sword, and is then surrounded by an angry army of them.
His prayer for deliverance is answered when he is turned into a tuna
also. He teaches them to use swords, and after some intrigues and
amusing adventures, becomes captain-general of their army and is
rewarded by the tuna king. He is finally caught in Spanish nets and
his skin is peeled off to reveal the man. He is not able at once to
convince his wife and the archpriest who he is, but the story ends
happily with a disputation at Salamanca where he makes the pomp-
ous rector look foolish.

Obviously this is not the same kind of tale as *Lazarillo*, though the
author has skillfully worked reminiscences of Lázaro's former life
into his new narrative. Reading it now, with our perceptions trained
to see a development of specific "picaresque" features which link
Lazarillo to *Guzmán de Alfarache* and Quevedo's *The Cheat*, this
Second Part appears irrelevant and absurd. If we put these later
works out of our minds, however, I think we can appreciate what
the original and the continuation may have had in common. In the
first place, the sequel pursues the original title's theme of "fortunes
and misfortunes." Lazarillo's upward movement is maintained—but
in a society of fish, not of men. Since he is not a true born-and-bred
tuna, his fish status is illusory. There remains the man within who is
simply temporising, making the best of a situation, acting a falsehood, even while he performs worthy feats of arms or rescues a tuna
friend from unjust persecution. In the second place, the fish-world
is an obvious reflection of the human world, with its kings and
courtiers, *alguaciles* and judges, generals and captains, streets and
squares, city and country, patriotism and conspiracy, its forms of

courtesy and respect. When Captain Licis is away, Lázaro will not visit his friend's wife without the company of the absent friend's brother. There are comic differences, too: the fish embrace by rubbing their snouts; tails, not hands, are kissed (and Lázaro expresses some repugnance over this). There are satirical comments on the corruption of power, and so on; Lázaro says that he was able to make use of the observations of the squire on serving the great with flattery, not truth. Both authors, then, have used distance as a means of obtaining a satirical perspective on the real social world; the original, by refracting the social vices of nobles and clerics through the meanest representatives, as we have seen; the continuation, by seeing the contemporary world in the guise of a kingdom of fish.

Even if these comparisons are fair, it remains true that the *Second Part* is in fundamental ways different from the original. The address to "Your Honor" is irrelevant, since the *Second Part* is not written in response to his command. The original *Lazarillo* doubtless owes something to the pseudoautobiography of the *Golden Ass* of Apuleius; the *Second Part* follows this model, and also some other tall stories of Lucian, much more literally. It could likewise be related to the literature of fantastic journeys, which proliferates in Europe about this time.

IX A Second Continuation

The next continuation, also called *Second Part of Lazarillo de Tormes*, was published in Paris in 1620 and is the work of an expatriate teacher of languages, Juan de Luna.[13] This is a joke, at least in part, because the author sets out to deny the truth of the previous *Second Part* and to set the record straight concerning Lázaro's tribulations at sea. Luna's Lázaro insists that after he was shipwrecked, he salvaged a treasure chest which he tied by a rope to his leg. He is rescued by greedy fishermen who have unwittingly cut loose the treasure, and who then decide to exhibit him in a tank of water, as a unique sea monster. The subsequent adventures, though they are of the kind that we commonly speak of as picaresque—practical jokes, brushes with the police, humiliations by low women—do not fall into shape as those of earlier writers do. It was an odd choice in 1620 to publish the continuation of a nearly seventy-year-old novel, when Alemán's *Guzmán de Alfarache* (1599 and 1604 plus Martí's spurious continuation, 1603), Cervantes' *Exemplary Novels*

(1613), López de Ubeda's *Pícara Justina* (1605), had appeared and Quevedo's *Cheat* had long been circulating in manuscript. Luna's work has some interest of its own—some fierce satire on the Inquisition, for example—but once the links with the original *Lazarillo* have been made, through the reappearance of the squire, the wife, and the archpriest, the rest of the novel reduces the protagonist to a plaything, cast this way and that by others who are malicious, greedy, or hypocritical.[14]

Although Luna's *Second Part of the Life of Lazarillo de Tormes* is not constructed on the same principles as the original *Lazarillo*, this is not reason enough for it to be dismissed as totally lacking in coherence. The original Lázaro had already reached manhood and achieved a position which was definitive, in the sense that it was apparently the situation in which the narrator found himself as he told his story. The writer of a continuation would have to make a break in the very act of starting *his* story, because the secondary figures in the earlier book were not like the characters in an adventure story, for whom new actions can always be devised, nor were they characters in the modern sense, whose psychology could be maintained and carried forward into new situations. They were part of Lázaro's boyhood experience, of his past, and as he related his encounters with them it was in the style of a boy's simple characterization of men. A new encounter, by the man, seeing and telling as a man, would be a revision (a re-vision). For all of such reasons, then, there would be no need—and no opportunity—for them to reappear in roles which made them continuous with earlier events. It appears rather that Luna has exploited, against all expectation, this completeness, this lack of loose ends in the formal structure of his predecessor's work. The ending of *Lazarillo de Tormes*—the protagonist's domestic arrangements—does contain a possible instability. We could say that the neatness is like that of an epigram: once we try to visualize it as a real human situation, it loses its balanced equilibrium. So Luna has Lázaro go off to join the Spanish campaign in North Africa. It is after the shipwreck and while he is being exhibited as a sea monster that he hears that the archpriest has made his wife pregnant. When he breaks free of his captors he brings a court action against the archpriest, but loses the case and all his money. This is enough to illustrate how Luna, perhaps recalling the "fortunes and misfortunes" of the original title, decided to develop the misfortunes. Nothing goes right for him. Every plan miscarries, every stroke of luck lasts only long enough to begin to taste sweet before it turns to bitterness. Finally in chapter 15, after a number of cruel disappointments, he meets a hermit and decides that he, too, will abandon the world. The hermit dies almost immediately, but Lázaro is adopted by the religious fraternity which patronizes the hermitage. He then finds that he is heir to a rich store of provisions and of money which the hypocritical hermit had amassed from the alms of pious visitors. Before long, the dead hermit's "wife," "mother," and "sisters" arrive, with his children. Hearing that he is dead, they claim his property. Lázaro, so as not to lose what he has only just gained, and looking forward to some easy female company, offers to marry the "widow." Of course, he is fooled once again as he submits to a form of ceremony which turns into a series of tortures from which he is finally happy to escape, naked but alive, into a church.

One could take Luna's continuation, then, as a reading of the final sentence of the original *Lazarillo* ("For at that time I was prosperous and at the peak of my good fortune") not in the sense of a firm and stable achievement, but in the sense of a balancing act which can topple at any moment, and which not only can, but is bound to do so. Luna shows us Fortune's wheel going over the top, the rapid descent from that peak. Lázaro's original laborious climb is matched now by a precipitous series of calamities. The first Lazarillo begins with his birth "in the river Tormes," and ends with his protection by the archpriest. The second has his "rebirth" from the sea, and ends seeking sanctuary in the church, where he is permitted to stretch out on a tomb, out of sight of the scandalized worshippers. He who earlier struggled to gain a place in the world, to gain "honor," and the clothing that would symbolize his "honor," is repeatedly stripped naked in Luna's sequel. Fortune is relentless in her pursuit of him, giving him nothing that she does not snatch away again almost immediately. This treacherous mockery, giving and snatching, is accompanied by torment and derision from those who look on.

As can readily be seen, this is a bitterly comic book, cast in a different mode from the original, yet not altogether inconsistent with it. What the first *Lazarillo* carefully assembled as a gesture of personal accommodation in a shifty world, Luna's destroys almost as if to make a demonstration in mechanics of forces in unstable equilibrium, or of the effects of building on sand. Nothing can be counted on. Even the squire, who reappears in Luna's book, shares the general debasement: he steals Lázaro's clothes (chapter 1). Many readers have protested that this is out of character.[15] Perhaps it mattered more to Luna that clothing becomes so important to the original Lázaro following his association with the squire. Del Monte has compared this book to Quevedo's *Life of Pablos the Cheat (Vida del Buscón)* in the extent to which the principal character is parodied and victimized by the author.[16]

Bearing in mind that Luna was a Protestant exile, it has been suggested that Lázaro's flight naked into the church at the conclusion of the book is an expression of the author's theology: "Luna's Protestant theology decrees that the only viable solution is an absolute dependence upon God's grace, and this is presumably the attitude adopted by Lázaro when he retreats into the church. . . ."[17] Such speculations are as risky as they are attractive, for in this instance Lázaro takes refuge in a Catholic church while Mass is being sung, thereby creating a scandal.

X *Late Variation*

Also in 1620 Juan Cortés de Tolosa, a little known writer, published *Lazarillo de Manzanares*, together with a group of shorter stories. The hero of this narrative is adopted by foster parents who remind us of those of Pablos in *El Buscón:* he is a thief and she a witch, and there are two daughters who are prostitutes. He splits the head of a person who insults his parents' good name and takes refuge in a convent. His mother finds him clothes for a disguise and sends him to study at the University of Alcalá. He serves a pastry cook and learns of the wife's liaisons and of the unsavory contents of the pies. The next master, a sacristan, also has a wife who deceives him and keeps Lazarillo busy with errands. The deceit of wives is common to a number of the episodes of this book, which makes it the more surprising not only that Lazarillo should be tricked by such false women (chapters 13–14) but that he finds no material for ironic self-reflection in this, or later, in his marriage to an ugly wife under pressure from a marriage broker. His adventures run from being adopted as assistant to a fraudulent hermit whose mock piety is so successful that the two live and grow fat in their rustic retreat, to tutoring the unmanageable nephews of a canon in Madrid, to being seized by robbers in the company of his young master when the

latter is escaping from his girl friend's house and made to go back
and help to rob it. At one point he decides to go to America to seek a
change of fortune, then changes his mind. However, the book ends
with a rich benefactor putting him on one of his ships going to
Mexico. A *Second Part* is promised.

This book follows the convention of autobiography, and adopts
the same mode of presentation as the original *Lazarillo*: an address
to "Your Honor" ("Vuestra Merced"). But the address is without
function, because this Lazarillo is not the same person, and we are
not given any reason whatever for believing in "Your Honor." We
are not told who he is, why Lazarillo is addressing him, or what he
wants to know. Parts of the story derive from earlier ones: the way
Lazarillo reacts to public comment on his parents recalls Quevedo's
Buscón, for example (see chapter 4). But the general impression given by the novel is not one of continuity in a tradition so
much as the inability of the tradition and this book to relate to each
other. The varied activities of the protagonist are so many external
adventures; they do not become experiences for him, coalescing
around a desire or a self-defining preoccupation. The book falls apart
when one looks for continuity of motivation, or significance in some
blatant inconsistencies of action or judgment. This is the kind of
book which appears to confirm the common notion that picaresque
literature is episodic, disconnected, without any more consequen-
tial ordering of events than is given by the night following the day or
a compulsive need to vary the action and the setting. The variety of
occupations goes from the honest to the fraudulent to the merely
odd. One of the curious features is that this is one of few such books
in which the protagonist never goes hungry. He is, on the contrary,
well fed and sleek. As Giuseppe Sansone has observed in the preface to his edition, this is a hero of satiety, not of hunger. Writing of
his stay with the sacristan, Lazarillo tells how the boys would pay
him with food or money to be allowed to ring the bell. As a result,
"what I ate on every occasion passes belief. . . . And what happend
with the old women? They would pay in gold for the holy bread, and
likewise so that I would open the church early. So, if the other was a
Lazarus because he didn't eat I was a Lazarus who might have died
of surfeit" (35). There does not appear to have been a second edition
during the seventeenth century.

CHAPTER 3

Guzmán de Alfarache

I *The Author, Mateo Alemán*

MATEO Alemán (1547–1615) was born in Seville of a father who was a physician and a mother who descended from a banking family in Florence. He is usually assumed to be of *converso* stock, though no documentary proof has yet been produced.[1] After studying medicine he attempted some commerical deals but got into financial trouble, then tried for a career in law. He was appointed by Philip II to investigate possible irregularities in the handling of state money in a village in Extramadura, and antagonized the local justices by overstepping the bounds of his authority, to such an extent that he was himself imprisoned (1583). Another royal judgeship nevertheless was granted him ten years later, to inquire into the conditions under which convicts were made to work in the mercury mines, then operated by the powerful German banking house of Fugger under contract with the Spanish throne. Although he did nothing beyond his powers on this occasion, his indignation was fired by the effects of that alliance of power and money on those who had no rights, and by the evasiveness that he found everywhere. He was, it seems, a man of fierce impatience, without administrative tact. His experiences as royal judge as well as the devious shifts to which he had recourse in his business operations contributed to his pessimistic outlook. There is little room for natural goodness in his world, unless it be joined with the supernatural grace and the heroic willpower of the saint. Apart from his one great novel, he wrote a *Life of St. Antony of Padua* (1604), a memoir of Fray García Guerra, archbishop of Mexico (1613), and a treatise on the Spanish language (*Ortografía española*, 1609).

If, as I believe, it is a mistake to read *Lazarillo* as if it required a moral self-consciousness in the reader in order to be semantically

41

complete, such a reading is inescapable in *Guzmán de Alfarache*. Where the author of *Lazarillo* interposes an ironic distance and leaves room in it for many unanswered questions, Alemán allows the reader very little room to move, and certainly does not intend that we go away with questions unanswered. He moralizes continually upon the action, and provides three prefaces to the *First Part* : "To the Ignorant" ("Al Vulgo"), "To the Wise Reader" ("Al discreto lector"), "How this Book is to be Understood" ("Declaración para el entendimiento deste libro"). In the second of these he tells us to "moralize as much as you like; there's a broad margin for it" ("podrás moralizar según se te ofreciere; larga margen te queda" [94]). It is clear that he did not intend us to be in any doubt as to the serious purpose of his book. *Lazarillo* begins with a prologue which mocks traditional prologues, with their erudition and their declaration that the reader who skims the surface will find entertainment, while he who penetrates beneath the surface will find a kernel of valuable truth. What Lázaro says is that he who reads may find something to please him, and he who does not go so deep may get some entertainment from it ("podría ser que alguno que las cosas lea halle algo que le agrade, y a los que no ahondaren tanto los deleite" [5]). Here it is the flippant narrator, Lázaro, who is speaking and disclaiming responsibility for any serious content at any level. The only general "truth" to be found is the cynical observation that it is a virtue in lowly men to rise, and vice in highly placed men to fall, as he observes in an aside to "Your Honor" (14). The author's voice is nowhere to be heard, for Lázaro has the first word and the last. In contrast, Alemán's three prologues are all in his own voice, and they tell us to distinguish between the acts of his rogue Guzmán and the reflections of his reformed Guzmán, the criminal-turned-author who wishes to make an example of himself. The point is reinforced by a pun: we are not to laugh at the tale *(conseja)* and miss the lesson *(consejo)* (94). In other words, we may moralize as much as we please, but the premises and the rhetorical frames are abundantly provided and are everywhere apparent in the book itself (see below, pp. 48–61.[2] Our only fundamental choice is whether to join the orderly ranks of the wise readers or the unruly mob of the ignorant and the stupid.

 Guzmán de Alfarache appeared in two parts, the first being published in Madrid in 1599 (though it had been completed in October,

1597) and the second in 1604. Each part is divided into books, and each of these into chapters. In the references that follow I, ii, 4, for example, will mean part 1, book 2, chapter 4.

In between these two there appeared a spurious *Second Part of Guzmán de Alfarache* (1602) by a pseudonymous Mateo Luján de Sayavedra. We shall consider this work and its effect on Alemán's own *Second Part* at the end of this chapter.

II *Summary of* Guzmán de Alfarache

After *Lazarillo*, the most obvious thing about *Guzmán de Alfarache* is its size: Alemán's two parts are, respectively, about five and seven times the length of the earlier novel. Such a difference of scale, of course, entails other qualities, too. But Alemán has followed the earlier writer's lead in making a fictional autobiography, and in creating a narrator whose career is scandalous and not meritorious. Also, like Lazarillo, Guzmán has parents who are far from being desirable models. In chapter 1 he tells how his father met his mother and seduced her in a situation contrived so as to fool her aged lover. In fact, the book begins with an extensive "prehistory" in which the narrator states that his father came from Genoa (and his forbears from the Levant), and tells of his business as a moneylender in Seville, involving shady deals in bills of exchange, and his capture by Algerian corsairs while pursuing a business partner who had run off with his money. In Algiers he conveniently became a Muslim, then easily converted back to Christianity when it seemed convenient to abandon his Algerian wife, steal her fortune in money and jewels, and return to Spain. Following the death of his father, Guzmán leaves home and, after some disagreeable experiences on the road, arrives in Madrid where he takes apprenticeship with a cook, and begins his career of thieving. Dismissed as the result of a shaming (though accidental) encounter with his employer's wife during the night, he first becomes a porter, then moves on to Toledo. Made rich by a successful swindle, he dresses expensively in the hope of catching the girls, but is swindled and made to look foolish. He joins up with a captain of infantry in order to travel to Italy and look for his rich relations, but loses money by gambling and finally becomes an embarrassment to the captain because of his gambling, his swindling, and his thieving, and is dismissed. When he arrives in Genoa and presents himself, penniless, to his rich uncle, he finds himself treated as an imposter, tossed in a blanket, and thrown out of the house. He then goes to Rome and becomes a street beggar, pretending to be disabled, and is given asylum and medical care by a cardinal, who is a model of Christian charity. Guzmán continually repays the cardinal's attention and patience by playing malicious jokes on his secretary, by gambling and other excesses, and finally he is dismissed. His next master is the french ambassador whom he serves as jester and as messenger in his erotic pleasures. When a lady who is annoyed by the ambassador's attentions has Guzmán exposed to public humiliation and ridiucule, he loses favor and is obliged to leave.

Part 1 had ended while Guzmán was still a member of the ambassador's household. It is marked formally by the telling of a story (Dorido and Clorinia) as part of an entertainment. Upon his departure, Guzmán makes one of his numerous and ineffectual resolutions to reform his life. He next becomes friends with Sayavedra, a perfidious companion who makes off with his baggage, with the help of other thieves. Shortly afterward, on the road to Florence, he meets Sayavedra who begs his pardon. They are then reconciled and enter into partnership. After robbing a merchant of a large sum of money in Milan, they go to Genoa where Guzmán plans to avenge himself on the rich uncle who rejected him previously. Posing as a wealthy noble with the aristocratic name of Don Juan de Guzmán, he is now received with great affection and respect, and pulls off another great swindle, then escapes to the port where a captain has a ship waiting for him. During the journey to Barcelona the ship is battered by a storm, in which his companion Sayavedra goes mad and throws himself overboard.

Back in Spain, Guzmán goes to Madrid where he tries some amorous adventures, but is fooled and swindled. In madrid he marries; his wife is a spendthrift, so he and his father-in-law join forces in ingenious swindles and keep their creditors frustrated. After his wife's death he decides to settle down and study for the church. He follows the full course of arts and theology at Alcalá but shortly before graduating he falls hopelessly in love, renounces his vocation, and marries. When his father-in-law is financially ruined he encourages his wife to become a prostitute; they move to Madrid but are expelled from that city, so they go to Seville where they find his mother is still living. The old mother does her part in finding good customers for her daughter-in-law, but their relations deteriorate until the latter runs away with a ship's captain. Guzmán now gains the reputation of an honest man, winning the confidence of a saintly old friar by the pretense of handing over to him a purse full of money which he says he found in the street, and asking him to announce it in church. It is claimed by Guzmán's mother who plays the part of a grateful old lady. The ingenuous friar collects alms for Guzmán and finds him a job as administrator of a rich lady's estate. He robs the estate shamelessly, passing the profits over to his mother, and lives with a female slave, until his depredations are discovered.

He is arrested and sentenced to one hundred lashes and six years in the galleys. He runs rackets in prison, but on the road to the port of Cadiz he and his companion Soto become bitter enemies. On board ship, Guzmán gains the favor of the boatswain (who is set directly over the convicts) and later of a relative of the captain, but Soto repeatedly gets him into trouble, so that he is flogged nearly to death. At this point Guzmán turns to God and feels the presence of grace, though his sufferings continue. When Soto organizes a mutiny, Guzmán informs the captain. Guzmán is proved innocent of the thefts which Soto had planted on him, and he is pardoned. The story ends here, with the promise of a third part.

That is a bare and incomplete summary of the principal incidents. Much has been omitted and not only from the sequence of events. There are four complete love stories told as entertainments in the course of the novel, for example. But more important than the narrative fragments which any such summary has to leave out, is the abundant nonnarrative material, the so-called digressions for which the book is famous. Guzmán, as he composes his life, offers many reflections on its episodes, on his motives as he recalls them, on the nature of life, man, society. He also recalls the states of mind, the doubts, hesitations, self-accusations that affected him at the time of the acts he is recording. The book is thus a rich counterpoint of action and commentary, a dialectic of "before" and "after," with what separates them—the experience of conversion—being the key to the whole. This experience has, like everything else, preceded the writing but, unlike everything else, it alone justifies the writing, because it alone allows Guzmán to see his life as exemplary and therefore writable. It creates in him the possibility of being the creator of his own life, on both the moral or ontological level, and also as an artist. Consequently, it is present throughout the book in the ethical and spiritual point of view of the writer, and in the quality of the reflections and judgments, of which so much of the book consists. That conversion justifies the writing, for Guzmán can see himself as a justified sinner. It is the impulse which launched his writing, and which sustains it. But to the reader this cause of which the book is the effect, is hidden from view. To us it is the terminus of the narrative, and only when we reach the end do we realize that here is the hinge which joins the actions of the story and the commentary on that story. When we reach it, we see that what was the end of the story is the beginning of the book.

III   *Time and Memory: Memory and Audience*

The adventures (the word looks almost too frivolous when set down next to *Guzmán de Alfarache*) are numerous and varied. The action has ranged over Spain and Italy, and many years have passed. Guzmán has married twice and spent seven years at the University of Alcalá. He tells us little about his first marriage, or even about his second, except what concerns his exploitation of his wife. His years at the university were passed over in silence except for the narrator's reflection on the shallowness of his religious vocation. Silences like these (or Lázaro's on his four years as a water-carrier) are evidence enough that the hero does not intend to provide a complete narrative of his life, that his goal is not a total recall of events. Neither Lazarillo nor Guzmán ever says "I forget . . ." or pretends that his memory is defective. On the contrary, the impression we receive is that everything *could* be recalled if that were necessary. Such is the consequence of the fluency with which Guzmán recalls the details of his elaborate swindles in Italy and the practical jokes in the cardinal's palace, or the ease with which he narrates long artistic stories heard many years before. The fact is that Guzmán, like Lázaro, is making a case for himself by stressing what he thinks we (or "Your Honor") need to know. The cases and the kind of self-justification are, of course, very different in the two novels.

It is interesting to see how Alemán begins his novel. *Lazarillo* began as a direct and apparently frank response to "Your Honor's" request for information: "Well, Your Honor should know, first of all, that they call me Lázaro de Tormes. . . ." Guzmán's efforts show no such directness:

> The desire that I had to tell you (inquisitive reader) the story of my life put me in such a haste to plunge you into it without first informing you of some things which it is as well to have clear (because not only are they essential to my narrative but they will also give you no little pleasure) that I forgot to close a side door by which some scrupulous logician might sneak in to accuse me of offending against the true order of argument, by not proceeding from the definition to the thing defined, and that before starting my story I didn't tell you who and what my parents were, and my uncertain origin. . . .(105–6)

That sentence is still not quite ended. What it reveals is not only Guzmán's desire to tell the story of his life, but Alemán's desire to imitate the problematic nature of writing, and of writing about oneself in particular. Those past tenses, "The desire I *had* . . . *put* me . . . I *forgot* . . .," etc., must mean that Guzmán has already been writing and has now gone back, either to add something about his parents, or to start over afresh. The involuted sentences show a writer who knows his life, but does not yet see it as a *story*. And the reason why he cannot yet move forward simply without self-conscious reprises, is that he has not yet conceived of a proper relationship with his reader, that unknown and inconceivable plural-singular "you out there." So Guzmán goes through the familiar (to any writer) search for a posture before that unknown fictional creature. Who is *his* reader? A prude? a voyeur? An idle skimmer of romances? A reflexion of himself? (but "Who am I?" he would have to ask). Later, the narrative will make clear what roles he has chosen for us, but not yet. Besides, he is also embarrassed at having to talk of his parents. He could pass over them—but there is too much gossip about them. So he is in a cleft stick: if he tells what he knows, he can be accused of failing to honor the Fourth Commandment; if he does not, tongues will wag because of his silence.

The rest of part 1, book 1 (six chapters in all) covers the events of no more than a few days, from Guzmán's decision to leave home (end of I, i, 2) until his arrival at Cazalla, no more than twelve leagues distant. This seems to be a disproportionate amount of space for so short a time. But this is a time which is crucial to our reading of the rest of the novel, no less important than the end. The one tells how and why he left home and began a life of deceit; the other shows him being redeemed from that life. Unlike Lazarillo, Guzmán is not given away as a servant, but decides to leave home, after the death of his father, and when money is running short. His father, it will be recalled, was an unscrupulous swindler, who was attractive to women and also, it is hinted, homosexual. His mother was skillful at playing men off against each other, so that Guzmán was never sure which one was his father. His mother's mother had been an even more accomplished whore, making each of two dozen men think the child was his (143). The family background, then, was as sordid as it was possible to be, but these were wealthy people, not like the miller and his wife in *Lazarillo*.

When Guzmán was telling of his mother's seduction at his father's estate, San Juan de Alfarache, he referred to it as an earthly paradise (129). Images of Eden and of an almost limitless guilt and corruption are joined at the beginning of the book. It is understandable that some commentators have taken Guzmán's subsequent life to be the result of an inescapable determinism imposed by his inheritance or by his nurture.[3] But as the allusion to Eden ought to make clear, what Guzmán is made to carry, in this extreme picture of degradation, is original sin, the propensity to evil which is shared by all humanity. Compare for example; "Everything has been, is and will be the same. The first father [Adam] was perfidious; the first mother a liar; the first child a thief and murderer" (355). The argument for determinism is contradicted by the ultimate reversal, namely, Guzmán's conversion, and also by much else. In particular, his motives for leaving home need to be read with particular attention. These are clarified for us in the last paragraphs of chapter 2. He is now entering the period of adolescence, and beginning to strut like a rooster ("Ya galleaba . . . ." [145]). In spite of the family's lack of moral principles, he is full of an impatient sense of honor, which impels him to go out and prove himself.

He immediately discovers that the world is not a bed of roses. He realizes that he has been spoiled, brought up on the best food, and so forth, and at his first stop at an inn he has to eat the most nauseous meal in filthy conditions, served by the slob of a landlady, and he vomits it up. He has spent a night in cold and hunger and will shortly be robbed of his cape, swindled, humiliated, wrongfully arrested, all in the space of two days, yet he will refuse to turn back. The reason is that same "honor," the fear of shame, of losing face if he retreats and has to admit that he made a mistake. He is not driven to Madrid by physical necessity, for he has told us that Seville, his home city, is full of opportunities for making a living and perhaps, a fortune (145). What drives him, then, is not a particular inheritance of restlessness or adventurousness, but the generic teenage desire to go out on his own, turn his back on his home, and prove himself. This generic motivation will be seen again in Italy when, on recalling himself at the age of twenty, he observes, "twenty years are a fearsome animal" ("terrible animal son veinte años" [599]). It becomes clear that Guzmán responds to motives which are not so much those of an individual youth with a psychology and a set of family circumstances uniquely his own, but of a representative youth who passes through characteristic stages in relation to family, world, and self. Explaining his impulse to leave the nest, he urges the reader, "Judge whether it was reasonable for a boy like me, who was starting to strut like a rooster. . . ." *A boy like me:* his conduct is referred to a model of what is typical.

This initial phase of the novel (part 1, book 1) is one of discovery. Guzmán discovers the outside world, and this forces him to make discoveries about himself. First, he exchanges the protection of home for filthy inns and rascally innkeepers. He discovers that justice seizes upon the weakest. He discovers in himself a proud attachment to his own first impulse and then an urgent desire to avenge himself upon the world which he can only satisfy vicariously. When a mule driver replies to Guzmán's story of the omelette made with addled eggs, and other nauseous food, with a sequel in which some students get even with that particular landlady, Guzmán is loud in his regret that he was not able to take his own revenge. Then, as the small squalid incidents follow one another, he is cast into a state of shock by the world's ugliness and degeneracy, but he steadily becomes aware that whatever enables the world to be what it is, is in him too. For example, wrongfully arrested and beaten, he rejoices inwardly when the tiresome muledriver is beaten worse than he is (191). These chapters show Guzmán as victim, but they also enable us to perceive the typical mechanism by which the victim will become predator. At this stage, the incidents are trivial and repulsive. They are also oppressive because they are repetitious. Through repetition, the world's malice is made to seem independent of individuals, therefore more universal and typical of the degeneracy of mankind.

As with this first book, so with the rest; we could say that it contains the whole novel, as the seed contains the plant. Let us now observe this process in the novel as a whole, on its various levels: action, motivation, the self awareness of young Guzmán as he lived those actions, and the commentary of old Guzmán as he sets them down.

IV The Level of Action

On the level of the narrated action, there is movement from place to place, and from person to person, which is maintained until the end. Guzmán is servant, porter, beggar, buffoon, soldier, counterfeit nobleman, adventurer, student, businessman, estate manager, convict. A man of guises and disguises, he was seen by his contemporary readers as *the* picaro, par excellence. More particularly he was perceived as a Proteus, a creature of multiple shapes, ceaselessly transforming himself:[4] "I was always busy seeking whatever was required for the trade that I now worked at [i.e., jester], so as to enlarge my scope and make other men's tastes fit my own. . . . And so, those gifts which Nature had denied me, I had to go after and acquire by cunning. . . . At that time, in the springtime of my years, everything went swimmingly, everything worked out, and I adjusted myself to everything. . . . It seems to me now that I must have been like the joker in the deck of cards, that anyone can use when and how he wants" (493–94). "Seeing these excesses in everyone else, I became like them. As I was among wolves, I learned to howl like a wolf. Everyone gambled, and cursed, everyone robbed and filched; and I just did the same" (297).

Observing such manifestations of changeableness, Stuart Miller has written that "the picaro revels in his variability, his abdication of self-determination. If society is a chaos of appearances, he will embrace that chaos by becoming totally 'otherdirected'. . . From other literature we have come to expect limits to adaptability, limits to the extent a character will sacrifice his personality. But in the picaresque there are no limits. The picaro is every man he has to be, and therefore no man".[5] It certainly makes sense to us to say that a person who tries to be everybody can have no personality of his own, but Alemán's readers understood the matter differently. For the poets who contributed prefatory verses to *Guzmán*, for example, he was a mirror of all mankind, and this appears to have been Alemán's intention also: "I think all men are like me, weak, easily led, with their natural passions—and some strange ones, too. . . . I think of myself the way you do of yourself" (481–482).

V *Motivation: Shame*

On the level of motivation for those actions and movements, the same few basic impulses are played time after time: honor, shame, vengeance, acquisitiveness, the pleasure of cheating. Again we are told that he did not return home, for shame (II, i, 1); again and again he dresses up so as to pass for someone of higher social rank. There is a disquisition on shame in II, i, 1, a concept *(vergüenza)* which is more extensive in Spanish, and includes embarrassment, the fear of how one will be judged by one's peers, and also doing something against one's better judgment because "I couldn't bring myself to refuse." Guzmán contrasts this with a more morally directed meaning: an aversion from doing anything base or shameful, "even when alone" (249). This "even when alone" divides the higher sense of shame as a register of the moral sensibility (shame 2), from the (shame 1) which is . . . social embarrassment, weakness under peer pressure, refusal to retreat from one's mistakes. Shame, honor, vengeance, are closely linked, and are the more dangerous because "higher" and "lower" senses are covered by the same word, and may be confused by the undiscriminating person. Cheating and acquisitiveness, on the other hand, can be more immediately damaging to others, but are soon recognized for what they are. They may intermix, of course, as when Guzmán naively presents himself to his rich uncle, hoping to gain both money and an honorable status for himself.

When he returns in part 2 and swindles the uncle of his treasure, Guzmán obtains both money and revenge. The desire to get rich by swindling, and the desire for vengeance are diffused throughout the novel. They also link the two visits to Genoa, many chapters apart, and as such provide motivation for a long-term narrative structure. The reflex from shame 1 (as humiliation, as wounded pride) to vengeance may be instantaneous, or it may plot a long arc in the desires of the picaro and in the design of the book. It could scarcely be accidental that the earliest disquisitions are on vengeance and shame, since these passions move the central character so greatly.

Moreover, Alemán inserts these commentaries into both levels of the narrative; one of them was delivered by a priest and is still recalled by Guzmán, the other is conceived by Guzmán himself. We should notice also that as we move from the level of personal narrative to concepts of value, shame 1 ("what will they think of me?") can be a perversion of (or substitute for) private virtue, as vengeance is a perversion of (or substitute for) public justice. And justice is one of the fundamental concepts of the novel.

Ironically, the lower sense of the word "shame" can protect the higher, for when Guzmán loses his fear of causing a bad impression (shame 1) he loses his shame 2 (self-esteem) altogether, and turns completely unscrupulous (I, ii, 2, 5). This is the point at which the narrator is conscious of having become a picaro, witness the chapter heading of I, ii, 2: "How Guzmán, on leaving the innkeeper, set out for Madrid and arrived as a ready-made picaro." Also, it is the place where the boy suddenly acquires the consciousness of freedom. Shame 1 has been eroded by hunger and necessity, and now he is freed from constraints. So he lives by begging, by gambling (and fixing the cards), and he eats at the monastic soup kitchen. In a mode which will become popular in verse and satirical song, he praises the "scoundrel's great life" (*la florida picardía* [258]).

VI   *Self Awareness*

On the next level—the character's feelings about his actions—there is another continuity from "then" until "now." It begins with the boy's tears as he spends his first night away from home, cold and hungry, and issues into the writing of the life story and its retrospective comments. I refer to the attitude of disenchantment (in Spanish, *desengaño*). The great swindles give him a feeling of exultation, but in the long term he is no better off, no happier, no more contented. On the contrary, he is continually looking for more victims, protecting his gains from his confederates, or losing them in gambling. His marriages end in death or desertion. His studies come to nothing because he falls in love and abandons his vocation. He has learned grammar, rhetoric, and the rest, but not how to discipline his feelings. The realization that this is so, that one's desires always outrun the ability to satisfy them, that at some crucial point we are the victim of our own nature, is part of this concept of *desengaño* which looms so large in Spanish literature in the seventeenth century. The Guzmán who is writing is, of course, the completely disenchanted man. He has been through it all, and as he relives the past in his writing, he covers his experiences with the reflections of disillusioned wisdom. He is *desengaño* incarnate. But the young Guzmán, in his moments of reflective anxiety, had also foreshadowed this entropy of the passions. His expectations that on leaving home he will meet success, that in Madrid he will automatically make his fortune (I, ii, 1; p. 250) or that rich financiers in Genoa will welcome a ragged sponger calling himself their relative (I, iii, 1) are promptly disconfirmed and give rise to some rumination at the time. There are also some dramatic images of this kind of defeat in the action itself. For example (in II, iii, 1) he is in the street making what he hopes will be seductive conversation with a woman who is on a balcony. He is annoyed by a dog and he goes to pick up what he thinks is a stone; but darkness is falling and what he grasps is excrement. As he recoils he scrapes his fingertips against the wall, and instinctively puts them in his mouth. He runs away pursued by the dog, and full of shame and fury (751–52). This incident requires no comment, for it conveys its meaning directly through the transformation of appearances. Its aptness for a character who himself is continually changing his role and his appearance is clear. It is necessary to reiterate, though, that this disillusionment with life is present in the earlier Guzmán, and is not exclusive to the reformed narrator. Of course, the familiar sensations of the passing of time, of change and loss, confirm the impressions of *desengaño*, and Alemán makes his hero pass more than once over the same track, in order to make the contrast. He returns to Madrid (in II, iii, 2), and notes: "Everything was greatly changed from when I left. The spice-merchant had disappeared without trace. The fields were now built on, the boys had become youths and the youths men, the men had become old and the old men had died. Squares had become streets and the streets were all very different and much improved" (756). In II, iii, 6, when he meets his aged mother in Seville, he will scarcely recognize her. She will be his last accomplice, and a treacherous one. The ambivalence is tersely presented: time carries us on toward decline and death, yet there is that thrill of new expectancy (the streets were different, "much improved").

Alemán's harsh view of the world is summed up in a striking image at the end of I, ii, 4: "Everything is in turmoil, everything restless, everything in confusion. No man stands by his fellow; we all live by laying traps for one another like cat and mouse, or like the spider that catches the snake unawares; descending on its thread and seizing him by the neck pinches hard, never letting go until it has made the kill with its poison" (280). This image of the spider and the snake is repeated in II, i, 8 with the maxim "Prudence is powerless to resist deceit." It also appears as an emblem in woodcut on the frontispiece of Alemán's books, with the Latin motto: *Ab insidiis non est prudentia.*[6]

VII *The Critical Debate*

Guzmán de Alfarache is the one among all the picaresque novels which has provoked most extreme reactions. In the seventeenth century, as far as one can judge, the work aroused enthusiasm, but not controversy. Its success was phenomenal: twenty-six editions of part 1 appeared between 1599 and 1604.[7] Alemán might complain (in the preface to part 2) that the reading public called his book *El picaro*, in preference to *Guzmán de Alfarache, Sentinel of Human Life,* but there can be little doubt that the combination of unedifying career and edifying commentary caused his readers no difficulties. Moreover, the translators of *Guzmán* into Italian, English, and Latin even went so far as to provide copious annotations on the commentaries in the expectation that the reader would not merely relish them but would wish to study them and relate their doctrine to the great writings of the Christian tradition.[8] Eighteenth-century taste, however, found the moralizing out of place; already the edition of Antwerp, 1681, had introduced the word "picaro" prominently into the title and later ones added the word "adventures" also.[9] A movement had begun which would emphasize action and plot at the expense of Alemán's commentaries. The famous French translation by Alain René Le Sage (1732) proclaimed itself to be "purged of superfluous moralizing" and from then on we find shortened versions being made in Spain also.[10] The justification for this procedure was that conformity to the "rules of taste," as these were understood in the eighteenth century, required that a narrative be continuous and smooth and that the narrator's reflections, if any, be confined to suitable pauses, and not allowed to break up the continuity, as happened frequently in the work of Alemán. Since Alemán had obviously written an interesting story, it became a matter of urgency to explain how a gifted writer had made such a gross "error" as to overlay his work with gratuitous moralizings. In the atmosphere of eighteenth-century intellectual enlightenment and nineteenth-century liberalism it was easy to be convinced that the real culprit was the Inquisitorial censor: only by including pious orthodoxies could the author expect to get away with some risqué adventures and some daring satire, it was supposed.[11] This opinion was current throughout the nineteenth century and is even now expressed occasionally.[12] Such a theory allows one comfortably to believe in the stupidity of the Inquisition's censors (whatever else they may have been, they were not stupid), and in exchange one is obliged to believe in the servility of Alemán (although his dealings with powerful financial and bureaucratic interests show that he could not be called servile).

In the last forty years, Alemán's work has become acceptable in its totality, but without any final agreement on its purpose or meaning. For Enrique Moreno Báez, Alemán is a proponent of Counter-Reformation ideology, and Guzmán is a demonstration of the theological argument that all men are depraved because they inherit original sin, but that even the greatest offender may be redeemed through the grace of God. Indeed, Guzmán does say that all men are equal in the evil they do (122, 343, 484, 620, etc.). In opposition to Moreno Báez, J. A. van Praag[13] has claimed that Alemán, an anti-Christian converso, was really making fun of orthodox dogma: an argument which has received very little support. However, a number of writers have sought to modify Moreno's position or to argue that the theological is not the only, or even the most important level on which to understand the book. While enthusiastically accepting Moreno's thesis, A. A. Parker sees Guzmán within the terms he himself sets for the picaresque as a whole, namely, the study of the social and moral implications of delinquency: "Whether one accepts or rejects the validity of its 'thesis,' there should be no denying that Alemán chose delinquency for a novel because it provided scope for an intelligent and earnest attempt to investigate the nature of moral evil."[14]

Against this claim for the theological-moral thesis, Alberto Del Monte has argued for Alemán as social satirist,[15] and Maurice Molho propounds both theology and satire: for Alemán, sinning is consubstantial with human existence, and the novel is less the story of a man than of a soul "caught in its pendulum-swings."[16] Gonzalo Sobejano rejects theological and moral interpretations and sees Guzmán's life as part of an educative purpose.[17] Edmond Cros examines *Guzmán* as a vast exercise in rhetoric applied to the themes of justice and mercy, and of the world as deceit.[18] Donald McGrady presents it as primarily entertainment, with part 2 being largely a *roman à clef*, though this makes it difficult to argue for artistic unity.[19] Edmond Cros, in a second book, accepts and modifies the suggestion of a *roman à clef*, reflecting stages in Alemán's own life.[20] For Angel San Miguel this story focuses as much on social criticism as on the moral progress of a picaro: its frame of reference is man's existence on this earth.[21] Finally, there are those readers who see Guzmán's father as a converted Jew; for them Guzmán becomes the projection of Alemán's own anguish and pessimism as a converso, i.e., as a person whose identity is constantly threatened.[22] It would be impossible to debate here all these various points of view. In a work as rich and dense as this it is possible for more than one preoccupation of the author to be held in solution.

Francisco Rico made an important distinction between the place of the religious motive in Guzmán's narrative as he writes, and its place in Alemán's complex purpose as *he* writes.[23] It is clearly central to Guzmán as he composes, or recomposes, his life as an exemplary warning for us, but through Guzmán's remembered experiences we look out on a world and a cast of characters which may interest us equally as parents, as consumers, as social critics, and in many other ways. When Alemán insisted on his subtitle *Atalaya de la vida humana* he made of his book a sentry alerting the reader to the dangers of the world we live in. The vision of the world which the book contains is, then, no less important artistically than the destiny of Guzmán and his displacement of success by the chance for salvation. If the world is a battleground or an arena and if, as Guzmán continually reminds us, we are in his shoes, then whatever we learn from his picaresque life is as important as what we learn from his chastened words. Each serves the other. The commentaries interpret *life*, and not just Guzmán's life. The career of Guzmán, a rhetoric of action, makes the commentaries plausible, gives them their sharp edge of particularity.

VIII *The Art of Confessing*

Guzmán refers to his narrative as "this general confession" (II, i, l; p. 484). Clearly, the incidental commentaries ("digressions," as they have often been called) are not superfluous if we remember that the book is supposedly written by a reformed convict of long experience and wide learning gained at the university as a student of arts and theology, who retained an uneasy conscience from boyhood, even as a successful swindler. Far from being a sop to the Inquisition, they are an essential part of Alemán's artistic intention.

They also help to make plausible Guzmán's conversion experience, by making us familiar with the mind of the "new" man over the span of many chapters. The commentaries provide a rich conceptual frame for the life of Guzmán: he is interpreting himself to us. The principal concepts are the possibility of salvation in any station of life (I, ii, 4; p. 275; cf. 1 Corinthians 7: 20), the freedom of the individual will (I, iii, 10; p. 437), and sufferings as a sign of God's favor (I, i, 3; p. 149; II, iii, 8; p. 891). Early in his narrative Guzmán says "The life of man is warfare on this earth" (*La vida del hombre milicia es en la tierra*). The phrase is taken from Job, whose fortitude in adversity may be seen as a model for the new Guzmán who is writing.

We could say also that to dismiss the "digressions" is to fail to see their necessity to the work's balance. It is a book of "before " and "after," with the conversion as the hinge at which the new is folded back over the old. Or it could be compared to a transparency showing contours or coordinates ("after") which is overlaid upon a confused map of experiences ("before") which then acquire shape and significance. Of course, the length of the book and the delay in time between parts 1 and 2 created one great problem for Alemán, because the artistic or structural justification of Guzmán the commentator has to be left until almost the last moment of the book. Not all readers find this delayed revelation acceptable, yet it is essential as the climax of the action where the outer and the inner man are at last harmonized, where the plot as story in action, and the plot as odyssey of the spirit are brought into conformity with each other.

Alemán certainly diminished the unfortunate effects of this delay by showing the young Guzmán to be uneasy in his life, as we have noticed already. He would have turned back if he had had the courage to accept his shame. Then there is the succession of ecclesiastics in the narrative who are consistently the only ones who show him charity and sympathy and share what little they have. In I, ii, 1 a poor friar shares his food with him and then departs along the road which Guzmán has just traveled, back toward Seville. He remarks "Those who had, and were able, were miserly and gave me nothing. I got it from a beggar and poor friar. . . . The others took no pity on my need. My good friar shared his food with me, and left me satisfied. If my journey had been toward Seville, like that blessed man, I'd have been set free, but our roads were in opposite directions" (253). The men of religion are not only exemplary persons, they are also signposts pointing for Guzmán's benefit, and each time he recognizes the message but is unable to respond to it.

There are many occasions, in part 1 especially, when the young Guzmán is aware that he is taking the wrong road, but is unable to act upon what he knows. So in his portrayal of Guzmán struggling to examine his motives even while still a boy, or tormented by his inability to do what he ought to do, Alemán makes us see that the depths of his personality are oriented toward the moment of final justification. To ask, as some readers do, how we can accept Guzmán's conversion as sincere when he never stayed straight before, is to have failed to read half of the book.[24] We should rather see, as Francisco Rico has seen (introducción, p. xlvi) the drama of a protagonist who in a desolation of the will passes by the favorable circumstances for self-amendment (e.g., in the household of the cardinal and at the university) and becomes regenerate precisely at the most unfavorable moment, as the victim of Soto's lies, and with everyone against him.

As Edmond Cros has observed, *Guzmán de Alfarache* is full of actions which evoke our ideas of justice. There are numerous lawsuits, accusations, denunciations, acts of vengeance (private "justice") jail terms, etc., and of course Guzmán is finally condemned to the galleys as a convict. There he experiences his conversion, and is finally reprieved. Thus, the "possibility of salvation" which is the whole theme for Moreno Báez, simply raises to a higher plane and subsumes the "dialectic of justice and mercy" which the book has been enacting.[25] The relation between the book and the reader appears to support this reading. Guzmán repeatedly addresses the reader in his commentaries advising him to see himself in Guzmán. The reader could well be the accused, but at the same time he is also called upon to judge, as receiver of this general confession. So there is a double identification of the reader with Guzmán: we share his guilt, and we are called upon to pass judgment, as he judges himself. These two involvements of the reader are articulated, once again, by that same hinge, the conversion of Guzman, since we simultaneously participate with Guzmán-picaro and meditate with Guzmán-narrator, our scapegoat and our interpreter.

Lázaro addressed the little memoir of his *Life* to "Your Honor".

Guzmán addresses his vast one to the reader, which is to say, to everyone. As sentinel, he is also mirror, since he reflects the world to itself. This intention is supported, as we have seen, by a psychology which is generalized rather than particular and idiosyncratic, and by a range of experience which makes him an epitome of mankind. He has no name until he names himself, just when he is about to go forth into the world (at the end of I, i, 2). But it is a fact that once this Adam-like stage is past, his life is his own, and that his acts represent a vitality and a wit which are his own. He is not to be confused with any other person in the story, and he is not allegorized. The more the individual experiences mount up, attended by much realistic detail and in recognizable surroundings—Seville, Madrid, Rome, etc.—the more concrete, specific, and individual Guzmán's life becomes. Naturally, this specificity and this concreteness can serve Alemán's purpose by making his portrayal of human nature and society plausible and convincing. But how can the author prevent the individual character and the concrete world he inhabits from running away with the reader's attention, to the neglect of everything else? If the reader skips over the commentaries, or weights his sympathy for the picaro and against the regenerate convict's point of view, is there any way that he can be checked? The answer, I think, is in two implicit underlying models, one existential and moral, the other narrative.

IX   *Structural Models*

The first is reflected in Guzmán's inner experience. A great sinner, deceitful, vengeful, and greedy for money and reputation, he suddenly is converted, and writes his personal testament, an epistle to the world at large. This pattern of a life turned about, converted, so that the new redeems, gives new meaning to the old, realigning it to a new goal, is a familiar one in the lives of Christian saints. The purest example of the "man made new," the earliest in time and therefore the prototype, is St. Paul who continually made of himself an example, a model fiction, and covered his life with commentaries in his letters to the Christian communities. And the young Guzmán's troubled conscience, which never left him, recalls Paul's famous words of self-analysis, "For the good that I would I do not: but the evil that I would not, that I do" (Romans 7:19).

The second model, the narrative one, is that of the wandering hero, exemplified in such grand figures as Odysseus or Aeneas.

Guzmán, like Odysseus, crosses the Mediterranean in search of his family origin, but in the event Genoa is only a stage in his career. His career eventually brings him home to Seville where he is reunited with his mother and joins her in lucrative swindles. If the pattern of heroic romance and epic usually imposes a return and a reintegration after long wanderings, Guzmán offers a close parody and travesty of that pattern. Odysseus is united with his patient wife Penelope, and casts out the evil suitors who had been consuming his estate. Guzmán is reunited with his unscrupulous hag of a mother and together they exploit his wife and fleece a rich widow of her estate. When Guzmán is arrested, tried, and sentenced, he does not see his mother or his money again. The geographical midpoint of his travels was Rome, and that is the halfway point in the novel, where the break between parts 1 and 2 occurs. In the middle section of the *Odyssey* the hero is washed up naked from the sea and is feted and treated royally by Antinous, king of the Phaeacians. In Rome, Guzmán is taken in his rags off the street and treated as a favored guest by the cardinal. But *Guzmán de Alfarache* also has something of a distorted mirror structure. Dismissed by the cardinal, Guzmán is employed by the French ambassador: they are both great and powerful, but if one is a prince of the church, great in charity, the other is a secular authority, great in malice and cynicism. Guzmán passes from being favored guest to hired buffoon and pimp, from free man who fails to be worthy of his freedom to lackey serving his master's caprice. From then on, the narrative may be said to have passed its turning point.[26] Guzmán will retrace his steps over the same road, meeting persons who recall previous ones (e.g., the two captains on his two sea crossings). The clearest example of the distorted mirror image occurs on the last stage of his life. He had suffered unforgettable humiliations at the hands of innkeepers in part 1, book i, on the road from Seville to Madrid. Now he marries the daughter of an innkeeper and travels with her from Madrid to Seville, and to new degradations.

In heroic narratives like the *Odyssey* or the *Aeneid* the wanderings and encounters serve to test and to temper the hero. He has to become worthy of that final restoration of harmony, that rejoining of ties and linking of the heroic past with a heroic dynasty in the future (Aeneas). Guzmán de Alfarache by his acts merely reiterates his unworthiness, going from shame to shame. Alemán has taken the familiar pattern and instead of making the hero's journey and return to his point of departure be the measure of his growth in character and experience, he makes it a completely closed system, a vicious cycle of iniquities. Guzmán does not escape until he is isolated on the galley, at sea, without location on the watery element that is no man's home, that age-old image of treacherousness, sudden changes of fortune, and inhuman vastness. The sea, more than any other thing, is a natural symbol for Guzmán's unstable life, with its lack of horizons. The journey-and-return pattern was traced out in precise locations; in this narrative appendix he is in no place that has a name. And yet it is here that he transcends his life, as Alemán the artificer transcends his generic narrative model. It is clear why Baltasar Gracián, in his praise of *Guzmán de Alfarache*, spoke of it as embracing "Greek invention, Italian eloquence, French learning, and Spanish wit".[27] In summary, the story and the commentaries should be seen as mutually necessary, not antithetical, and the book may be entered from either side, *conseja* or *consejo*, the tale or the message. We may see it either as Guzmán's life, expanded and universalized by the intellectual framework of the commentaries, or as an expatiation, a rhetorical assault upon human life illustrated by the experience of the picaro.

Finally, a few words about the interpolated stories. The first, *Ozmín y Daraja* (I, i, 8) is set in the kingdom of Granada at the time of the final campaigns of Ferdinand and Isabella. The noble and chivalrous Moor Ozmín becomes separated from his love who is in Christian territory, and the story is the record of his efforts to be reunited with her. In *Dorido y Clorinia* (I, iii,) 10) a bloody tale of rejected love turned to hate, Oracio poses as his favored rival and when Clorinia extends her hand through an opening in the wall, he cuts it off. Dorido's vengeance against Oracio is no less violent. In II, i, 4 we are told how the fifteenth-century constable of Castile, Don Álvaro de Luna, had offered a reward to the one of his companions who could tell the love story in which he exposed himself to greatest danger. Finally, in II, ii, 9, after the death of Sayavedra, one of the sailors attempts to console Guzmán with the story of Dorotea, a beautiful, virtuous, but poor lady who survives abduction, false accusation, and imprisonment (against a background of arson and mysterious deaths) and finally is reunited with her husband.

All these stories are told by characters in the book in response to an occasion. The first, *Ozmín y Daraja*, is related by a priest and reveals the triumph of resolution and love against adversity, jealousy, and malice. All the others, as can be seen even from these brief summaries, show violence engulfing virtue, passion wreaking insane destruction, sexual love as merely a dangerous male sport. Even in *Ozmín y Daraja*, the longest and most attractive of these stories (Mozart used it for an opera), the hero has to resort to disguise, deceit, feigned, identity; ugly scenes develop between the noble protagonist and the common villagers, some of whom are killed. Ozmín is imprisoned and sentenced to death. He is released only by royal pardon, that is, by bending justice. As others have pointed out, the chivalresque air of gallantry and noble endeavor do not override the general impression given by Alemán's fiction, namely, the grim, quarterless struggle that is life, the measureless greed, cruelty, and deceit of which human nature is capable when left to itself.[28]

X   *The Spurious Guzmán Part Two*

In 1602 there appeared a *Second Part of Guzmán de Alfarache* written by a certain Mateo Luján de Sayavedra. This was a pseudonym, and in the course of his own second part, Alemán unmasked the author as Juan Martí, a Valencian lawyer. Alemán accused him of plagiarizing his manuscript as he was preparing it for publication, but there is not really much in Martí's continuation which could have been written by Alemán. The first third, perhaps, may be derived in some measure from what Alemán had written, but the rest has almost no action, and the picaro himself is no longer recognizable as the same person. There is an increasing predominance of anecdote, moralizing, and irrelevant commentary as the novel proceeds. By the end of the book the protagonist has become a sneaky snatcher of capes by night, so that the reader loses interest in his actions at the same time as those actions are buried under digressions which have little or no organic relation to Guzmán or to one another. A notable example is the three chapters (book 2, chapters 9–11) which are taken up by a Basque servant's argument proving that all Basques are hidalgos by right of birth. What this book does is confirm the fact that for many readers a picaresque narrative was one in which the "hero" was continually on the move, and gave a vicarious glimpse into the houses of the rich, the taverns and dens of swindlers, and the dark alleys where crimes were committed after dark. The narrative and psychological tension between "then" and "now" is absent. The moral dimension of time and change is displaced by one thing merely following another, and Alemán's grand epic journey by a shapeless itinerary in which progress follows caprice rather than art. The new perspective from which Alemán's Guzmán views and reviews the past is missing, for although Martí's creature is sentenced to serve in the galleys, the experience does not change him. Indeed, he is freed, and promises new adventures for his third part.

CHAPTER 4

Quevedo's Pablos, El Buscón

THE *Life of Pablos the Cheat* (*La Vida del Buscón llamado Don Pablos*), by Francisco de Quevedo y Villegas (1580–1645), is usually known simply as *El Buscón*. Its author came of an aristocratic though not a wealthy family. In fact, he lived as a child in the royal palace where his mother was a lady-in-waiting and where his father and his grandparents had also served. Throughout his life he remained acutely sensitive of his noble birth and descent from pure blooded northern Christians, and of the preeminence that he thought he deserved by virtue of his lineage, the services rendered by his family, and his intelligence. He became intolerant of upstarts whose origins were obscure and who perhaps inherited semitic blood, and detested those who were inferior to him intellectually but who, nevertheless, mastered the art of gaining and wielding power. Quevedo's career as diplomat and secret agent gave him opportunities for intrigue, but also exposed him to counter intrigue which led ultimately to his fall from favor.[1]

There are some artists whose imagination is so dominated by their temperament and by their posture before the world that these qualities show in all their work, however diverse it may be. Swift, with whom Quevedo has been compared, was such a writer. Quevedo wrote voluminously in a number of different genres: his love sonnets have a range and an energy and a rhetorical power which reminds one of John Donne, and his *Política de Dios* is a pious and disillusioned treatise on government which proclaims Christ to be the only model for kings. He also wrote many hundreds of other verses, satirical and scurrilous ones especially. The *Visions* (*Sueños*) which he composed over a long period of years are little masterpieces of satirical fantasy, in which the thought can as easily follow the possibilities offered by puns and other verbal ambiguities as other more realistic devices. Yet at the risk of oversimplifying we could say that both the piety and the bitter fantasy share a common root in

64

Quevedo's profound uneasiness with life and the world as he found them. The Catholic monarchy of Spain was above public reproach, as was to be expected in that age with its identification of church and state. But Quevedo was close enough to the center to have no illusions about the human failings of the king, the venality and hunger for power of his ministers. The continual conspiracies and petty treacheries of those who sought to rise in power were matched only by the slanders and false accusations and other forms of tyranny exerted by those who had authority and jealously defended it.

The great intellectual brilliance of Quevedo, his familiarity with philosophy and theology, his mastery of languages (Latin, Greek, Hebrew, French, Italian) gave him a superiority which in the *Política de Dios* he could make appear as the elaborate oblation of a servant to the king and his minister. But when not constrained by respect for higher authority, his aggressive, sardonic, and disdainful temperament found direct expression in the other prose works. From this point of view, it is interesting that in *El Buscón* he created an upstart as central figure in the story, and interesting too that he deals so ruthlessly with his creature.

The conservatism of Quevedo was not only moral and social, but artistic also. In 1631 he published an edition of the poems of Fray Luis de León (d. 1591) as part of an effort to oppose the new style of poetry represented by Don Luis de Góngora (whom he vigorously satirized). So when he wrote a novel in the picaresque manner, he chose to follow the brevity of *Lazarillo de Tormes* rather than the discursive length of *Guzmán de Alfarache*. In other respects also Quevedo models his book more closely after *Lazarillo*. However, it would be misleading to suggest that *El Buscón* is like *Lazarillo* and unlike *Guzmán*, because it is different from each of them and in some ways it is a travesty of both of them. On the best evidence, it was a youthful book, completed perhaps during 1604 though not published until 1626, by which time it had circulated in many manuscripts, and in more than one version.[2] The author apparently took no part in the publication, which was done on the initiative of the bookseller Roberto Duport who supplied a preface which until recently was believed to be Quevedo's.

I   *The Plot*

Pablos' life begins in even less auspicious circumstances than does Lazarillo's or Guzmán's. The father is a barber and a thief who trains his other small son to pick customers' pockets while they are being shaved. The mother is a whore, a procuress, and a witch. Later, we find that he has an uncle who is the public hangman. Not surprisingly, he decides early in his life that he would like to rise out of this pit, and begins to entertain fantasies of becoming a gentleman ("Siempre tuve pensamientos de caballero desde chiquito" [18]). So when his parents quarrel over which of them he should follow, he persuades them to send him to school instead. Unlike his picaresque predecessors, Pablos goes to a local school, then to boarding school, then to university. He also has as his companion a son of the local nobility, named Don Diego Coronel. At the University of Alcalá, Pablos' conduct becomes so scandalous (petty thieving, practical jokes, and frauds) that Don Diego's father has them separated. From then on, Pablos is on his own. He returns to Segovia, where his father has been executed and his mother is held by the Inquisition, and where he hopes to inherit some money. His uncle gives a party for him which becomes a drunken brawl, and he leaves for Madrid to seek his fortune. On the road he meets a certain Don Toribio who looks like a gentleman but is discovered to be dressed in patches, and who instructs Pablos in tricks for living without spending money. In Madrid he joins Don Toribio's group; they get into fights with genuinely poor beggars, and a few days later are all in prison.

After some repugnant experiences in the jail with homosexuals and bullies he bribes his way into better living quarters, then ingratiates himself with the prison governor and gains his freedom. He tries to win the marriageable daughter of the owner of his lodging house by posing as a wealthy business man and landowner. His plans are spoiled when he slips on the roof on his way to her room, is caught by a lawyer, and nearly jailed. He makes his escape and has another attempt at a profitable marriage, using secondhand clothes and a rented horse. Again, he has the girl and her mother deceived, but this time he is recognized by his former companion, Don Diego Coronel, who is the girl's cousin. A fall from a borrowed horse and some other unfortunate incidents indicate that he is in fact a charlatan and Don Diego, having his suspicions confirmed, gets his servants to beat him after dark.

He has been finally defeated in his ambition to become a gentleman. He is looked after by a woman who runs a lodging house, but these comforts are short-lived because she is arrested for performing witchcraft. From now on, Pablos is continually on the move: begging as a false cripple; kidnapping children in order to claim the reward for rescuing them; acting in a traveling company; writing bad plays; swindling at cards; joining the hopeless lovers of nuns at the convent railing. Finally, having reached Seville, he goes on a drunken rampage with his companions, and they kill some police and have to take refuge in the cathedral. They are ministered to by the local whores who smuggle them out. Pablos, not wanting to spend his life being hunted by the police in Seville, takes ship to America, and here his story abruptly ends. Viewed thus, as a succession of states and occupations, the life of Pablos is not particularly interesting. But this is not all there is in the book, because Quevedo has built his narrative around an obsession with status which shows in all his climactic experiences. Such experiences are not conveyed in a summary of episodes, and we must now turn to them and give them their due weight.

II *Childhood Shame*

As we have seen, Pablos is given parents of such extreme depravity that he could not fail to want to escape from them and their example. He begins, therefore, to curry favor with the schoolmaster, to be the good boy of the class (thus earning the right to punish the others), and to court the friendship of the noble Don Diego. For example, he gives Don Diego his favorite toys. Nevertheless, the world seems to conspire to remind him of his shameful parents: he is pelted with vegetables while riding a horse in a fiesta, and recalls his mother's shameful progress in the Inquisitional procession when she, too, was pelted. He breaks the head of another boy who calls his mother a witch and a whore; when he tells her, she merely says that he ought to have found out who had spread the story, and that such things should not be said, even if true. The motivation to hide his origins and to better himself socially has been established as a dominant pattern of behavior.

This desire for greater social respectability, however, appears to be an aspect of a more fundamental desire for acceptance, which Pablos shares with real people, although it does not always harmonize with the social aspiration. An example of this is to be seen in the episode of the repellant initiation that he has to undergo as a new arrival at the university and more particularly in the consequences of this episode. After his extreme physical humiliation (of which more later) he determines to "do as others do" (75) and even to be a bigger scoundrel than all of them. He now has the respect of the rowdier students, leading them in escapades of a daring, ingenious, and semicriminal kind—the preeminent accomplishment of Pablos during the remainder of his career. During the interval between the spitting episode in the college quadrangle and the worse events of that same night when Pablos is beaten in the dark and made to wallow in others' excrement, Don Diego had observed "Open your eyes, they're out for blood. Watch out for yourself, there's no mom and dad here" (67). True, but a cruel remark in its way, because Don Diego has been taken under the protection of friends of his father but does not exert himself to protect his servant and companion. It should be clear to Pablos by this time, as it is even to the modern reader, that the tradition of patriarchal concern on the part of noble masters for poor servants does not operate in his world, and that the noble can escape humiliations of the more brutal sort by use of money and authority (even if he may be cynically exploited as a green youth momentarily, which happened at an inn on the road [book 1, chapter 4]). It is equally obvious that Pablos's desire is to acquire precisely that kind of respect. For the time being he must content himself with a different kind. He is not able to join those whom he would like to (represented by Don Diego), so he joins those whom he cannot defeat on his own side of the social barrier. In fact, he is so notoriously successful in leading student hooligans that Don Diego's father makes his son sever relations with him (I, 7).

At the same time that Don Diego hears from his father that he must dismiss Pablos, Pablos receives a letter from his uncle which gives an account of his father's death. The uncle Alonso Ramplón (in English he might have been called Harry Gross, Bill Crude, or Dick Low) is the public executioner who has just executed him, and he describes the death as if it were an exemplary, heroic one, and invites young Pablos to come and claim his part of the inheritance. Thus Pablos is back at square one, separated from his savior Don Diego, and confronted again by the shame of his parents. This is characteristic of Quevedo's tendency to overdetermine the reader's response to his story, a tendency which can be more easily accommodated to the satirical fantasies of the Visions (Los Sueños) than to extended narrative.

III   Final defeat and loss of shame

In the following chapters the hero runs away from his uncle and his drunken companions and goes to Madrid, still harboring the intention to make good and leave his shameful origins behind him. Once again Don Diego, who has disappeared from the narrative during thirteen chapters, is brought forth to be the agent of punishment, of the definitive separation of the protagonist from his goal. Once again the unbridgeable social distance between the two characters has been demonstrated. This time, however, it is not measured by the immunity which rank and wealth confer, but by the brute force which rank has at its command. Don Diego does not soil his own hands in punishing Pablos. By exchanging cloaks, he ensures that some men who were waylaying him because of an affair with a wench (*una mujercilla*) beat Pablos instead, and later the same night he has his own men set upon him with cudgels and slash his face with a knife (III, 7; pp. 239–41). The parting wound is verbal: "That's for being a lying lowborn crook!" ("¡Así pagan los pícaros embusteros mal nacidos!"). The social rejection, "low-born," is literally the last word spoken on behalf of Don Diego.

This fall of course puts an end to Pablos' ambitions, though it is not yet the end of the story. The remaining few chapters, however, are not really like the earlier ones, although some of the incidents are not very different in nature. After his injury he wakes up in the bed of an old woman who is a prostitute and who is soon arrested on suspicion of being a witch. He then becomes a beggar, a false cripple, a kidnapper of children in order to claim the reward offered for their recovery, an actor, a poet, and playwright who steals other men's lines. After courting a nun he becomes a sharper again and, as we said before, his career in Spain ends after his attack on the police in a drunken brawl. All of these incidents are told with a cynical verbal wit which is characteristic of the whole book, but they are all brief, trivial, disconnected. Since Pablos' long-term expectation that he can recreate himself by rising to a new social level where his parents are unknown has been destroyed, they represent his inability to escape, and the futility of his life.

To say that these incidents represent inability to escape and futility requires some justification. As he concludes his book with the resolve to leave Spain "to see whether I would change my luck with a change of scene and a different country," he adds the final comment: "But it was for the worse, as you will see in the second part, because no one improves his situation who only changes his location and not his life and habits" (III, 10; p. 280). At the moment when he writes his story, Pablos apparently perceives his life as being at an impasse, needing a new direction. One can only say "apparently perceives" because Pablos, unlike Guzmán de Alfarache, hardly ever reflects upon himself or explains his actions. On the few occasions when he does so (his decision to stop being a timid and well-behaved youth and to outdo them all in mischief is an example) the change is so obvious that, as his own narrator, he has to give some attention to causal links. Pablos is predominantly a teller of actions without much thought for self-explanation, but Quevedo has other devices for disclosing such judgments, notably devices of repetition and self-parody.

After Pablos has been cast down by Don Diego from the heaven he seemed about to enter, he no longer has any hope of identifying himself with the nobility of blood and rank. The immunity of Don Diego at the time of Pablos' humiliations and the fact that his privileged companion did nothing to protect or favor him, were strong signals that his ambition was futile; the two worlds of plebeian and noble might touch, even merge, but each man carried a different charge which would inevitably cause the one to move with assurance and the other to founder as soon as he crossed the invisible line. This final disaster confirms the warning of asymmetry that went unheeded or imperfectly understood in the first, for if Don Diego is above the torments of Pablos' world, Pablos is conversely unqualified for the blessings of Don Diego's.

Pablos once more joins the crowd. The events which follow his expulsion from the gates of paradise until his departure from Seville in the last lines of the book reverse the set of relations which appeared earlier, following the death of his father. During that period (book 2) he turned his back upon his uncle in disgust, lost his money to a card-sharping friar, (II, 3) made merciless fun of Don Toribio and his tattered pseudo-gentlemen (II, 6), pilloried the versifier who wrote for blind street singers (II, 2–3), ridiculed an *arbitrista* ("armchair reformer," called a "projector" in England at the same period) and a student who claimed to fence by mathematics (II, 1). In other words, though he may cooperate with Don Toribio's companions, he remains intellectually aloof and sharply satirical, evaluating stupidity and hypocrisy for what they are. In the second period, however, he poses as a card-sharping friar, is given new life after his injuries by a woman who is cast in the same mold as his mother, becomes a false cripple in order to beg, writes trivial verses at so much the line. Finally, he takes part in an attack on the police after a drinking bout with a collection of toughs who recall to us the companions of his uncle. He also becomes an actor who observes how writers will "steal another man's play and after adding some stupid rubbish and throwing out the good lines they claim it for their own"; but quite soon he is writing rubbish of his own and ham acting to the top of his bent. These are the devices of repetition and self-parody by which we catch Pablos doing something which he had ridiculed or detested when it was previously done by someone else, and which we may read as signs of futility and disintegration.[3]

There is little agreement among commentators about the value or even about the seriousness of this novel. In its short span it contains set pieces like the proclamation against bad poets (II, 3) and the earlier brilliant verbal, and typically Quevedesque invention of the Licenciate Cabra and his boarding school for boys (I, 3). Each of these pieces is an example of virtuosity and the latter is less a portrait than a sequence of verbal squibs all of which translate visually the *ideas* of starvation and of stinginess. "He was a blowpipe in holy orders: only his length was generous"; "His whiskers had turned pale with fear of the neighboring mouth which seemed to threaten to eat them from sheer hunger; I don't know how many teeth were missing and I guess he had dismissed them as idlers and good-for-nothings: his gullet [was] long as an ostrich's, with an Adam's apple that stood out so far it looked as if it were forced to go in search of food . . ." (22–23). The joining of visual distortion and verbal fantasy to produce a caricature really has nothing to do with the novel, brilliant though it is. It is clearly the work of Quevedo the author, rather than of Pablos the narrator, and it employs a technique of reducing human forms to mere aggregates of things, which has more in common with some of the *Visions* than with the rest of *The Cheat*.

The episode of the initiation of Pablos among the students is clearly important, since it marks a decisive moment in his career. "Look out for yourself," says Don Diego (67); "Watch out" says Pablos to himself (73). Some kind of an awakening has apparently taken place, but Pablos has really gone from one delusion to another, from impossible aristocratic ambition and shame for his origins to undisguised mischief and identification with his tormentors. This alternate denial and embracing of the world he detests, implying an alternate affirmation and rejection of innocence, is the pulse of the work, as we have seen in the way the episodes are put together. Not that the innocence is truly innocent; a corrupt naivety calling itself innocence would be a better description. But as soon as we think we detect a moral or psychological unity in this novel, Quevedo's manner of composition—his pursuit of singular verbal effects, or his throwaway unconcern with consistency of narration[4]—make us suspicious of our readiness to discover significant structures. The direction of the story is clear enough, of course: Pablos was determined to rise but has finally sunk as low as the parents whom he wanted to escape. What is the meaning of this ironic sequence? Was Quevedo tracing the career of a protagonist whose choices are morally confused and therefore self-destructive? Or is this decline the satiric means by which the self-consciously aristocratic author continues to persecute an upstart who had ideas of rising above his station? The answer, probably, is both of these, with the youthful satirist exploiting the vogue for moralistic fiction as an instrument at the same time as he parodies it. In what follows I shall attempt to explain this view.

We have seen that the episode of Pablos' initiation by the students at the University of Alcalá leads to his adoption by reaction of the life of a cheat and a hooligan, and to his separation from Don Diego. The episode is also important in itself and has been a topic of controversy in recent years, since T. E. May's article of 1950[5]. May draws attention to the following details: the phrase "I'm not an *Ecce Homo*" addressed by Pablos to the owner of his lodging (a Morisco) when he returns covered with the shower of spittle that the students inflicted on him; the students' derisive "This Lazarus is ready for resurrection, to judge by the stink" ("por resucitar está este Lazaro según hiede") when he appears among them (63); Pablos' inexplicable falling asleep in the middle of the day and his being awakened by Don Diego's voice saying "This is another life," and imagining that he is dead.

These details form part of a whole sequence of unmotivated suffering and humiliation. Putting all this together, May sees a deliberate travesty of the mockery and crucifixion of Christ not, of course, so as to ridicule the Christian story, but in order to measure the inadequacy of Pablos. Whereas Christ is the model for accepting unmerited suffering as an inescapable condition of life, Pablos' rage and shame and his decision to revenge himself upon society are a symbolic rejection of salvation and of God's presence in individual lives. The idea that life continually challenges the individual to incorporate Christ's pattern of suffering into himself in order to transcend suffering, is familiar doctrine to Christian believers. May does not mention that ceremonies of initiation, rites of passage from one stage of life to another, and of access to an inner group of initiates, commonly do employ the forms and symbolic language of death and rebirth. Quevedo, a member of the knightly Order of St. James and a classical scholar, could hardly have been unaware of this. There are difficulties here, though May's essays provide a rich context of argument. One question which will remain is: supposing that the initiation at Alcalá reproduces the familiar pattern of the scapegoat suffering at the hands of the malicious crowd, and supposing we agree that a picaresque frame does not per se inhibit the formation of the religious image, is this what Quevedo is really about?

We might suppose that Quevedo, being fascinated by the success of both *Lazarillo* and *Guzmán de Alfarache*, felt the impulse both to outdo and (being Quevedo) to travesty them. Impatient at the pious longueurs of *Guzmán*,[6] he reverted to the scale of *Lazarillo*, and created a character with whom the reader would *not* empathize, in a world which is repulsive and grotesque. Like Guzmán, Pablos sets out on his life beset by material filth and human malice. Then, in the most repellent of these episodes, Don Diego announces to him a "new life." Pablos takes up the same phrase a little later, but Pablos does not mean what Don Diego means, and neither of them means what Guzmán meant. Quite to the contrary, Quevedo has made disdainfully clear to the reader that if there is one thing Pablos will not do it is reform or experience a spiritual conversion. This point is made so early in the book that the author can devote the rest of it to destroying his "hero" in a stream of puns and verbal conceits. Much of the flippant verbal display is quite inappropriate to Pablos, but entirely in keeping with Quevedo's own style of incessant destructive wit.[7] Guzmán asserted that when God loads you with sufferings, that is a sign of his favor toward you. Very well, Quevedo will reject Alemán's art, his sermonizing, his double-decker hero, and beat down his own Pablos, all with one blow.

Guzmán crosses the invisible barrier between the reprobate and those who have responded to the touch of divine grace. In doing so he, like Christ and the Christian martyrs, has to give up all hope of material restoration and social acceptance. Pablos never gives up these hopes, though he is completely crushed in his search for salvation through social ascent. It is precisely in the space between the aristocratic world of Don Diego and the smelly, violent, cheating, vulgar world of Pablos that Quevedo has fixed his uncrossable barrier. But in reality this is also the space which in the world of Quevedo the author is most vulnerable and is the object of most anxiety. His satire would not need to be so fierce if he were not aware that the unthinkable, the unpardonable, was in fact being done, the invisible boundary being crossed, the taboo violated. Men who made money did marry dowerless girls of noble blood, or buy land so that their children might have the means to claim noble rank, and the old nobility always found in this movement a threat to the social order.

What is so fascinating in this book is the presence in it not only of the transgressor and the invisible hand that punishes, the picaro who breaks the taboo and the author who manipulates the social reflex which crushes him, but also a third, highly ambiguous figure: one who has crossed (or whose ancestors crossed) the forbidden boundary with the connivance of the highest authority, and who has changed his appearance with the change of identity. He is no longer recognizable by those on the outside of this favored precinct. He is the converso Don Diego Coronel, whose ancestor the Jew Abraham Seneor was baptized Fernán Peréz Coronel under the aegis of Queen Isabel the Catholic on June 15, 1492.[8] In 1589, members of this family were engaged in a suit to prove that they were legitimate descendants, entitled to protection under the privilege granted to their ancestor, and other members of the family were contemporaries of Quevedo at the University.[9] Quevedo's other writings contain plenty of anti-Semitic jokes, and he belonged to that type of persons for whom once a foreigner, always a foreigner. It is the high point of his ruthless wit that one who made the passage to hallowed ground (to Quevedo's continual discomfort) should pronounce sentence and carry it out against him who tries to cross over without a powerful protector and with relatively little money.

The Coronels had had the good fortune to cross over the boundary, to be "born again" in a social sense as well as in the sense of being converted to Christianity. Faced with the distasteful choice, Quevedo would have found a high-born Jew less unacceptable than a low-born mongrel Pablos. But the converso's rejection of the "lying low-born picaro" is in the vein of the author's blackest humor. So is the fact that Don Diego hides his hand when striking at Pablos, just as the accusers who denounced suspected Jews to the Inquisition could hide *their* hands. When Don Diego warned Pablos,

"Open your eyes, they're out for blood" and again "Watch out . . .", this was not just the advice of the moment, but the voice of generations of conversos, many of whom identified themselves with their tormentors, and whose immunity from persecution might prove illusory at any time. Here is an irony of different levels: keeping one's eyes open meant one thing to Pablos, another to Don Diego, and yet another to the intolerant xenophobe Quevedo.

John Donne's phrase, " 'Tis all in peeces, all cohaerance gone;/All just supply, and all Relation," applied truly enough to the social world of the early seventeenth century, in which money could buy the plumage of the noblest birds and confuse the sight of a man who expected clear, simple, traditional boundaries. Quevedo, at least in *El Buscòn*, found a form for his unique blend of arrogance and anxiety toward the cauldron of ambitions, shame, and protean energies which seethed beneath his feet and, too frequently, burst into view. His marionette Pablos, twitching in obedience to only two strings—rejection of the past, and desire for social acceptance—and wearing the protective grimace of aggressive servility is hustled through familiar scenes which are assembled into provocatively burlesque sequences. Meanwhile, the ventriloquist Quevedo, with careless insolence, lets his own undisguised voice accompany the actions, and the sharp glint of his spectacles flash continually in the shadows of the mock stage.

Francisco Rico has called *El Buscón* "a book of genius . . . and a very bad picaresque novel."[10] This is a dramatic way of drawing attention to the intense *verbal* organization of the book, for the thematic structure, as we have seen, is dissolved into the acid of the author's linguistic play. On this level it becomes impossible for us to discuss a book whose composition is often inconsistent, whose characters are caricatures, whose occasional moralizings are double-edged, whose view of society—bakers who put flesh from hanged men into pies, police who subvert justice, lawyers who do nothing without bribes, everybody stealing, cheating, lying—is no more *real* than is the empty space which surrounds Vladimir and Estragon in Beckett's *Waiting for Godot*. It is impossible to discuss here in English because, as Raimundo Lida has said, "what lends relative unity to the *Buscón* is the incessant jokes, puns, and sarcasm, the profusion of details: ridiculous, sordid, and at times even dazzling."[11]

CHAPTER 5

Cervantes

M IGUEL de Cervantes (1547–1616), the author of *Don Quixote*, published a collection of short novels or long short stories in 1613 under the title *Exemplary Novels (Novelas ejemplares)*. Two of these, *Rinconete and Cortadillo (Rinconete y Cortadillo)* and *The Dialogue of the Dogs (Coloquio de los perros)*, depict vagabonds and low life, and are commonly called picaresque. A third, *The Illustrious Kitchen Maid (La ilustre fregona)*, has among its principal characters a youth who escapes from home to go bumming in the tuna fisheries of the south coast. Each one of these stories shows in its own way Cervantes' awareness of picaresque literature, and yet it certainly cannot be said that he was simply picking up and continuing the new vogue. Indeed, his own versions of picaresque reveal an attitude which was critical of the way Alemán in particular handled the human material.

In *Don Quixote*, part 1, chapter 22, the knight meets a group of convicts who are being led in chains across country to the port of Cartagena, where they will begin to serve their sentence by doing forced labor in the galleys of Philip II's navy. The most heavily chained and closely guarded among them is a certain Ginés de Pasamonte, a notorious criminal, who tells Don Quixote that he has written his life story "with these very hands":

"It is so good that *Lazarillo de Tormes* had better watch out, and so had all others of the kind which have been or ever will be written. I can tell you that it deals with true facts, and such fine and entertaining facts that no invention can compare with them." "And what's the book called," asked Don Quixote. "*The Life of Ginés de Pasamonte*," he replied. "And is it finished?" asked Don Quixote. "How can it be finished," he replied, "if my life isn't finished yet? What is written goes from my birth to when they sent me to the galleys this last time." "So you have been there before?" said Don

Quixote. "I spent four years the other time, for God and king. I know the taste of hardtack and the lash, and I'm not grieving too much about going because I'll have the chance to finish my book there and I have many things left to say. . . ."

By this time (1604?) *Lazarillo* was clearly seen as belonging to a literary family. The fascinating thing though, about this conversation, is that the speaker is an arrogant rogue who is famous as a criminal but who wants to shine as a writer, and he makes the claim that truth is better than fiction. And in answering the knight's inquiry "Is it finished?" he lets slip his egregious literal-mindedness: raw facts taken from life, unprocessed, are superior as entertainment, not only as documentation. But there is a contradiction in his words as well, because when he says that the facts of his life are "fine and entertaining," the word which I have translated as "fine" (*lindas*) does mean loosely, "nice," "fine," but also and more specifically, "pretty," "attractive." So the rough fellow who makes the no-nonsense claim in behalf of the unvarnished truth is also implying that the absence of varnish is *attractive*. Now, every reader of Aristotle (*Poetics*, chapter 9) or of his commentators knew that the aesthetic truth of poetry was of a philosophical kind and therefore superior to the merely factual truth of history. Truth to an idea is of a higher order than a mechanical truth to the facts. But Ginés de Pasamonte, who has said that his book will follow his life faithfully from beginning to end, has put facts in first place. Then, by claiming attractiveness, he also asserts something of that very aesthetic value which he has disdained. But we are dealing with autobiography, and it would have been impossible for anyone to argue at that period for the purely aesthetic value of autobiography. A life, whether one's own or another's, was of importance only insofar as it was a model to be followed or as it illustrated pitfalls to be avoided. The convict does not say that his *Life* has any such exemplary value, but only that it is truthful and entertaining. The reasonable inference is that he finds himself to be enormously interesting by the very fact of his existence and assumes that others will also. The resulting book would be either boring or egotistic sensationalism, or both. The final point to notice in this interview is that Ginés de Pasamonte says he wrote his book "with these very hands" ("por estos pulgares"), indicating thereby the creative, craftsmanlike aspect of writing, though the Spanish ("thumbs" rather than "hands") betrays an oafish pretentiousness in the writer. A life does not become writing by any natural process; what is written may be true, but it is also necessarily contrived and arbitrary. The convict probably did not give much thought to this, and indeed a gross naivety forms part of Cervantes' portrait of the man. His craft would no doubt be what one might expect from one whose hands are all thumbs.

When we recall that Guzmán de Alfarache became a criminal and was sent to the galleys, after which he wrote the story of his life, we may begin to suspect that a literary judgment has been embedded in this exchange of words. And when Ginés de Pasamonte (each component of whose name contains the same number of syllables as Guzmán de Alfarache together with some other phonic similarities) refers to Lazarillo de Tormes by name, but leaves Guzmán among the anonymous "others," that judgment can only be one of disdain. The history of Don Quixote is being related by Cervantes on the authority of "documents," "informants," and the "wise Moor" Cide Hamete Benengeli; in other words, it is subject to an infinitely flexible system of controls and to a play of perspectives. That of Ginés, like that of Guzmán, allows the reader no controls, no ironic perspectives, since the story is contained within the subjective viewpoint of the protagonist and may simply follow the current of his self-pity, his excuses, and his self-congratulation. The object of Cervantes' criticism is, in the words of Harry Sieber, "open-ended frameless imitation of experience without the structuring control of art."[1] One does not have to agree that this is fair criticism of either the *Lazarillo* or the *Guzmán*; in fact, the authors of both these works display extraordinary virtuosity in fragmenting the unitary first-person viewpoint and introducing ironic perspectives. But when a writer is creating a new literary space for his own, radically different work, we cannot expect him to stand aside and admire those whose methods appear to deny his own. Finally, before leaving this incident, we should note that each of Ginés de Pasamonte's fellow convicts tells his story with the most outrageous bias, and in the most innocent-seeming euphemisms: one is sentenced for being poor (i.e., for not having money to pervert the course of justice), another for singing (i.e., for squealing under torture), and another for an act of love (i.e., for embracing some moneybags), and so on. With a wit that is characteristically absorbed into the fabric of his novel, Cervantes makes his hero's rash and foolish action in releasing the convicts result from just such "uncontrolled" narrative.

I Rinconete and Cortadillo

This is the story of two boys, both runaways, who meet by chance at an inn on the road south to Seville. Their names, like Dickens' Mr. Gradgrind, Trollope's Mr. Slope, or Galdós' Benina, are informative. The younger, Diego Cortado ("Cut"), learned to cut cloth from his father who was a tailor and then graduated to cutting purses. Pedro Rincón ("Corner"), the older, accompanied his father who was a pardoner (a *buldero*, like Lazarillo's master in chapter 5) until one day he ran off with the money. They both gloss over their activities with witticisms and speak with enough tone and ceremony to deceive the landlady of the inn into thinking they are young gentlemen, since she only hears their voices. But they do not deceive each other, since they have the evidence of their eyes. Thus from the start the use of language to disguise reality and to create a counterreality is an essential part of this story.

They cheat a mule driver at cards before taking a free ride to Seville with some travelers, whose luggage they rifle on the way. In Seville they first take up the job of carrier in the market, and practice some skillful thieving by sleight-of-hand and tongue, before they are noticed by the scouts of Monipodio who runs the rackets in Seville. They are told they had better join his "brotherhood" and are taken to his house which is the center of operations. There they observe the comings and goings of burglars and spies, pimps and prostitutes and are introduced to the great Monipodio himself, "the coarsest and most misshapen barbarian in the world"(165). There is a moment of alarm when the lookout reports that the chief magistrate is coming down the street, and they all fly through doors, windows, and skylights, but the danger passes and calm is restored. This part of the story contains various comical and grotesque episodes in the domestic life of Monipodio's gang. Monipodio examines the two new boys to judge their experience, aptitude, and character, and acquaints them with the rules of the society. He then "renames" them Rinconete and Cortadillo. A complaint is brought by a constable who is friendly and useful to Monipodio, that a purse has been taken from a sacristan on his beat. Monipodio orders whomever has it to give it up; it was taken by Cortado in the city before the boys were approached by Monipodio's scout, but he hands it over anyway, and is commended for his outstanding behavior. An old woman brings a stolen basket of linen, drinks an enormous pot of wine, then goes to the church to perform her devotions. One of the molls comes in and raises a howl that she has been beaten by her man, and the affair is commented on among the group. Impromptu singing and dancing follow as they beat out a rhythm on a shoe and a broom, and Monipodio rattles two bits of plate between his fingers. There is also a business meeting at which Monipodio, who is illiterate, has Rinconete read from a book the various contracts for beatings, knifings, and so forth which have been accepted, and calls for reports from those of his company who have been entrusted to carry them out. The boys are assigned to their pitch in the city and told to report back the following Sunday. Here the story ends, with Rinconete's critical reflections on what they have seen and heard, the strange contradictions in the lives of these thieves and hired thugs, and his determination to leave. However, "led by his lack of years and experience, he continued there a few months longer," and so a continuation is promised: "we leave for another occasion the story of his life and miracles and those of his master Monipodio, as well as other events from that academy of infamy, all of which will be worthy of close attention and will serve as an example and a warning to those who read it" (Clasicos castellanos ed., p. 218).

   Rinconete y Cortadillo (an earlier draft of which existed about 1604, at the time, perhaps, when Quevedo was writing and circulating *El Buscón*), differs in some obvious ways from the model structures of *Lazarillo* and *Guzmán*. It is not autobiographical in narrative technique, and there are two picaros, not one. There is no expressed desire to convince the reader, real or imagined, of anything by means of the narrative. There is no hunger, and no prolonged period of service with masters. Life is not presented as a journey through different professions and levels of society. Although the journey structure is preserved, it is radically altered in range and importance, and whereas Guzmán starts his life in Seville and moves away, Cervantes' two boys have Seville, the city of opportunity, of riches, and of crime, as their goal. The anguish of Lazarillo (physical at first and then social) or of Guzmán (spiritual and existential) has no counterpart here, for these boys are cheerful, footloose, and unconcerned. They are more curious about, even entertained by, the sordid, grotesque, and brutal world they find themselves in, than nauseated by it.

If Cervantes was interested in embodying a personal conviction in this story, it is perhaps that personal convictions are best not embodied in stories. He does not identify the writer with the internal narrator, as the earlier fictional autobiographies do, nor does he make his narrator into a ventriloquist's dummy, as Quevedo frequently does. The world of *Rinconete and Cortadillo* is not Lazarillo's tight little contrivance for excusing his life of soiled clothes, soiled words, and soiled relations, nor is it Everyman-Guzmán's confession of self-betrayal against a panorama of universal deceit and ruthless greed. Finally, the story is not even of novel length, but is one short story among others in the collection of *Exemplary Novels*. (In recent years the original Italian word *novella* has been brought into use to designate a narrative which is not a novel, but more extensive than the anecdote or isolated experience which make most modern short stories. That is the sense in which Cervantes used the word *novela* in Spanish, and I shall employ it when referring to such works.)

The action of *Rinconete and Cortadillo* falls into two parts. In the first, the two boys are the object of attention, and in the second they are bystanders watching the strange underworld of Seville and its operations. The first part can be further subdivided. At the beginning, the narrator presents the location—the inn on the road to Seville—and describes the two boys: it is a static scene with two portraits. Then they begin to talk and things happen. Each one gives a brief summary of his life, and they agree to become companions, and the first victim of their collaboration is a mule driver who is left furious, having been cheated by them at cards. The next phase is the journey to Seville which confirms their partnership and their career as swindlers. Less brutal than the criminals they are to meet in Seville and amusing as they may be, they do steal from their benefactors without scruple. Unlike Alemán, Cervantes does not make us feel the boys' consciousness at this point. We never know whether they rob on this (or any other occasion) "because it's there" or for some other motive. After a brief spell in Seville as free-lance carriers and pickpockets they are taken to Monipodio, and from then on, as we have seen, they become observers, only momentarily called upon to speak, and for most of the time standing in the same

relation to the underworld as we have stood to them. They themselves have two functions in the story: they are the protagonists, or
double protagonist of the first part where they speak and act and
move, and in the second part they are the agency by which we are
granted access to Monipodio's world.

If we now turn our attention to the narrative distance, that is, to
the degree of directness or indirectness of the discourse, we find
Cervantes making a number of shifts in this comparatively short
work. Beginning with static presentation, using accumulated visual
details, Cervantes suddenly changes to direct dialogue. The narrator who tells has given place to the prompter who adds the "he
said," "the other replied" while for a number of pages the actors
speak for themselves. Thus the prehistory of the boys is told by each
to the other, not by the narrator to the reader. Also, each one is
using a language not his own in order to create a posture before the
other: "What land is your honor from, gentle sir, and whither, pray,
are you traveling?" "What my land is, I know not, Sir Knight, nor
whither I am traveling" (136). They continue using this ceremonious
style until their questions and answers are concluded. The matter of
their exchange is that they are both runaways, which we can well
believe, but the circumstances in which they left their parents may
or may not be as they say, because their miniature autobiographies
are part of this stylistic game which continually changes, from self-
pity to self-congratulation, to sententious consolation, to speculation
on the mysteries of Providence. In little more than a page, we have
gone apparently from a standard omniscient narrator to one who is
unable to guarantee the truth of what he is allowing us to hear. And
yet, if we look back over the opening page of description, we find
that the narrator was less absolute in his knowledge than appeared.
There is vagueness about the boys' age: "perhaps fourteen or fifteen
years old, neither one exceeded seventeen" (133). The contents of
the bundle carried by one of them are noted because, in the words
of the narrator, "this was revealed later" (134), and the boys' names
are not given until they themselves declare what they are. Thus we
have a narrator who, it appears, is adhering closely to the order in
which events were disclosed to him, is saying nothing for which he
does not have authority, though we never know what that authority
is, and scrupulously refrains from inserting personal opinion into his
story.

The final paragraph of the story, which points to the incongruous piety of the gang, their laughable ignorance, the curious reign of authority there, and the corruption of justice in Seville, comes from the observation of Rinconete, so that judgments are made to originate within the story itself, independently of the narrator. Needless to say, this is a clever device on Cervantes' part, and there are indeed external judgments: the narrator underwrites Rinconete's observations by commending his intelligence and sense, for example (216). But he later restores his neutral balance by informing the reader of the lad's lack of years and experience which caused him to remain there longer.

It remains to point out that the scenes in Monipodio's headquarters are not simple reportage, and the earlier sequence with the boys was not just a way of leading into them. Two things especially strike one about this part of the story. The first is the deliberate resemblance between the brotherhood *(cofradía)* of Monipodio and a religious fraternity. They are thieves "in the service of God and all good people" (159). Monipodio himself is their "superior" *(mayor)* and "father" *(padre)*; the newcomers are required to spend their first year as novices on probation; they turn their back on their family and "the world," and are rebaptized, so to speak, with new names appropriate to their profession. In the case of Rincón and Cortado, as we have seen, their surnames are suggestive enough already, and Monipodio simply grants them the diminutive suffix of familiarity. All stolen goods become the common property of the community and are shared out among them.

There is a code of loyalty to the extreme of martyrdom for the brotherhood, and an expectation that they will spend their days under persecution, and end them on the gallows or as convicts. They also observe religious obligations in their peculiar way; to their devotions at a particular shrine they attribute miracles (such as the ability to withstand torture); many of them abstain from stealing on Fridays, and they do not have "conversation" (as they say) on Saturday with any woman whose name is Mary. One of the whores of the company expects that the toil and sweat she expended in earning twenty-four reals will be counted against her sins hereafter. Hence this company presents a double image of the "respectable" world. As "underworld" it has an organization, forms of allegiance, and even titles which are a mirror image or parody of the "upper" world. At the same time, its members adhere to the forms of religious respectability of the world outside.

The second thing to notice is the place that language has in creating this separate world. When Rinconete and Cortadillo met the established pickpocket who was to lead them to Monipodio, they were immediately puzzled by the words he used. The thieves' slang is a badge of separateness, of course, but it is more than that, because it has eliminated the value and judgment-laden words which belong in the outer world. A horse thief in their language is a *cuatrero*, or "trader in four [legs]," for instance. Their jargon, like that of any in-group, filters out the words which express the outer world's disapprobation, and substitutes its own. Thus, the words for thief, gallows, flogging, the various forms of torture and punishment, as well as the goods of their profession are replaced by others of their own coinage. By means of language, the criminals of the story have invented a reality which, examined more closely, is simply the reality of the conventional world turned back to front. This is a looking-glass world where thugs and crooks and whores are models of devotion and piety, where Monipodio orders Rinconete not to name the person who is to be exposed to public humiliation because that would be needlessly to compound the dishonor. The sentiments and expressions of these people, in short, are highly respectable, and they run their affairs with care for efficiency, for discipline, and for law and order. Similar tributes have been paid by honest citizens to the *mafia*, from Al Capone to our own day.

The reader is bound to experience a backlash as he reads *Rinconete and Cortadillo*. If the underworld is so close a parody of the hallowed institutions of the conventional world, is conventional society more like Monipodio's antisociety than we normally admit? The question is similar to that which is raised by Don Quixote's madness, as the presence of the knight precipitates or uncovers endless follies among the allegedly sane, both in the conduct of their own lives and by their interference in his. If, in the great city of Seville (remember that Cervantes gives us a real city, not a make-believe one) justice and crime are so intimate, if police and criminals are so mutually dependent, and if hoodlums can be hired to attain the satisfaction of someone's honor, we may reasonably wonder about our society and about the seriousness with which words like law, respect, honor, are commonly used.

This is where the double role of the boys becomes most clearly effective. Their pretentious use of language at the beginning of the story is an attempt to transform the reality of their origins and their rags; they do not deceive each other, but the mistress of the inn was "amazed at the rogues' good breeding, because she had been listening without their noticing it" (145). In Seville they will find such linguistic transformations practiced in so thorough and systematic a way as to represent the consciousness of a community. The linguistic virtuosity of Rinconete and Cortadillo is engulfed and annulled by the language of the tribe, which also stamps them with new names. At the same time, they cease to be actors in roles of their choice, because in pursuing freedom they have encountered a conformity and a servitude as confining as any in the "legitimate" world. Cervantes has found a form in which moralizing and explicit statement are unnecessary. By showing us that the language of the underworld is a fully developed form of the boys' language, he also makes us see what they see as spectators there: namely, their own future, themselves absorbed and institutionalized, no longer orphans because "father" Monipodio watches over all his children.

II   The Dialogue of the Dogs

The last two pieces in the collection of *Exemplary Novels* are *The Deceitful Marriage* and *Dialogue of the Dogs* (*El casamiento engañoso y coloquio de los perros*). Their titles are joined because the two stories are interlinked. The most obvious way in which they are related is in the fact that the narrator and principal character in the *Marriage* also presents the dogs' conversation which he claims to have overheard. The relation between these two is far too complex to be dealt with in a discussion of Cervantes' response to picaresque literature. Yet, we cannot isolate this latter aspect of his creation from everything else: part of his critique of previous picaresque writing is to be discovered in the new combinations that he makes as well as in the way he changes the internal structure of events.

At the gate of the city of Valladolid two friends meet (Clásicos castellanos ed., p. 176); one is Ensign Campuzano who is just leaving the Hospital of the Resurrection, and the other is Licentiate Peralta. The ensign has been receiving treatment for syphilis (strict diet and sweating) and is now stepping weakly toward the city. This meeting is the occasion for Campuzano to tell of his courtship and marriage with a Doña Estefanía. Each party to the marriage was deceiving the other as to fortune, and they both deceived themselves about how much truth they could tolerate. The marriage fell apart abruptly when the ensign discovered that his wife was not as comfortably off as he had supposed, and she, fearing his revenge, disappeared with his jewels. But his jewelry was false too, and the only tangible gain he could show was the syphilis. This is Campuzano's story, but he goes on to say that while he was lying in bed one night during his treatment he heard the two hospital guard dogs talking at the foot of his bed, and recorded their conversation. Peralta is understandably skeptical, but Campuzano insists that his friend read the dialogue as he transcribed it from memory. Peralta agrees to do this so long as he is not expected to believe in its literal truth.

The *Dialogue of the Dogs* is the content of Campuzano's manuscript which Peralta reads. The two dogs Cipión (which is Spanish for the Roman name Scipio) and Berganza find that they have suddenly acquired the miraculous gift of speech, without knowing how or why. The best way they can think of to use it is for each to tell the other the story of his life. Berganza begins, and it is agreed that Cipión will tell his story on the following night if he is still able to talk, but in fact Cipión's story is never related. Berganza tells of the various masters he served, from the brutal butcher at the meat market, to the shepherds who kill and steal sheep and tell the owner that a wolf is to blame, to the rich merchant who lets him go to school with his son, and a number of other masters. The strangest episode is his encounter with the witch Cañizares who tells him he was born as one of a pair of twin boys to another witch but that a third witch had turned them into puppies. There are other episodes and adventures after this, until Berganza, badly wounded while serving in a company of players, decides to leave that kind of life. Seeing Cipión travel the streets in the company of the pious and humble man who begs on behalf of the hospital and acts as its custodian, he ingratiates himself with them, and is accepted as Cipión's companion.

This *Dialogue of the Dogs*, as is obvious from the title, is not a fictional autobiography. It does not purport to have been written by the subject, unlike the other novels which we have discussed. It is not an uninterrupted narration, either, because Cipión intervenes, questions, criticizes, offers advice. The two dogs discuss the world of men, their experiences, their motives. Cipión counsels Berganza to avoid idle gossip and censoriousness, and not to chase random trains of thought, not to add tails to his tale until it looks like an octopus (251), to control his urge to preach and pass judgment. It is

Cipión who advises brevity and who declares that there are two kinds of story: those which are entertaining in themselves, and those whose charm is in the manner of telling.

Thematic relations between the two stories, *Marriage* and *Dialogue,* are not difficult to find.[2] Berganza's relation of his life from puppyhood to the present is a series of encounters with deceit, fraud, perversions of judgment and intellect. What the ensign had experienced in his disastrous marriage with Estefanía, both as victimizer and as victim, is expanded, generalized into the experience of the world at large. When Berganza expresses his shock at finding that the shepherds were not the guardians of the sheep but their butchers, Cipión moralizes: "the trouble is that it is impossible for people to get along comfortably in this world unless there is mutual trust and confidence." And yet new questions arise immediately we make this connection between the two stories. Is the dog's view of human society a partial one, or can we say it is truly representative? The persons Berganza encounters exploit and deceive each other (the thieving butchers, the shepherds, the scheming constables, and so on), but we can expand the notion of trust and say that they also betray a trust in the positions they occupy, the roles entrusted to them. In the witch, and to a lesser degree, the crazy inmates of the hospital (the poet, the alchemist, the mathematician, the projector) the faculties of reason and judgment are betrayed. The witch, of course, is a special case and her importance in the story lies outside the rather limited perspective we are adopting here.

At the beginning of their conversation, the dogs commented on the legendary fidelity of their species (211). If, among humans, dogs have come to represent loyalty and trust, does this imply that such virtues cannot find any suitable embodiment among the humans themselves? The family with whom Berganza finds contentment for a time is that of the silk merchant (235–58). But his very employment as guard dog is owed to the fact that the security of the merchant's home must be defended against the world outside. And he loses his position because the security of that home is being taken advantage of by a servant who lets her lover in at night and bribes the dog to keep quiet. When Berganza tries to do his duty the pair attempt to poison him, so he runs away. He had enjoyed a brief period of happiness when the merchant's son used to take him to school, but he had to be left at home because the boys in the class attended to him instead of to their lessons. Through no fault of his own he is expelled from the school where the Jesuit teachers patiently attempt to "train up the tender shoots of youth so that they will not be diverted or take a wrong turn on the road of virtue, while also teaching them letters" (242). The presence of Berganza shows how easily the students are diverted from their own learning to teaching the dog tricks. While the Jesuits attempt to make men ("humanity" in the Renaissance sense of both moral training and liberal studies), the boys are attracted to an animal. They watch him "crack nuts like a monkey" and distract him from his natural dogginess in one direction, while he tries to improve on it in another direction (by attending to the class). It would be difficult to deny that Berganza in his conversations with Cipión has learned more "humanity" than most of the boys in the school.

Are we to conclude that the Jesuits are really wasting their efforts, and that the sons of rich merchants will become frivolous pursuers of amusement, or perhaps that their training will remain as external as the tricks learned by a dog? That while the merchants themselves amass their fortunes (which are not acquired by trust and plain dealing, we may suppose) their sons will learn to hide their origins, to ape the nobility at court, substituting one kind of manipulative skill for another? As Cipión reminded us at the outset, when a husband and wife were represented together in sculpture on a shared tomb, it was customary to place the figure of a dog at their feet, representing fidelity. The premodern consciousness relied upon emblems, exemplary models of this sort, and upon proverbs which also ensure the continuity of cultural experience. The proverbial and emblematic significance of the dogs plays against the vision of the real world of men as the dogs themselves have experienced it. Men do not hide their true faces from animals as they do from one another, so that a dog's eye view of the human world cannot be a flattering one.

Cervantes' ironies, however, are never as simple as this. The continual presence of the dogs as narrator and critic ensures that we never lose sight of the contrast between the positive values that the dogs symbolize and the real nature of the human world upon which they depend. But there is another incongruity to be seen between this same affirmative value of the dogs as symbols of loyalty and trust, and what these particular dogs do and say. As they talk they reveal some very human weaknesses. They find fault, accuse each other of being longwinded or hypocritical. Cipión tells Berganza to keep to the point as he narrates, but when the latter says, early in

his story, that something puts him in mind of the encounter with the
witch, Cipión would like him to jump to that part immediately (230).
Then again we may reflect that dogs, even more than horses and
mules, are far from being "natural" animals. They have been bred
by men for their use, so that a dog is in some ways as dependent
upon man as a child is.

If Cipión and Berganza appear at times to be hypocritical, in-
gratiating, that is how their relationship with man requires them to
be, such are the conditions of their survival. The faults of the dogs
(and they are recognizably *human* faults) may make them unreliable
commentators, as some recent critics have asserted, but this is not
the same as being unreliable observers. One can go too far in dis-
crediting the dogs' view of the human scene, by seizing on their
criticisms of each other and by following up the pun left lying in our
path by Cervantes when he has Cipión say that they may be accused
of being cynics (251).[3] Berganza, after all, has risked his life in
standing up for his masters' interests, and has taken some beatings
for protesting against injustice, which is more than can be said for
the humans in his story.

The episode of Berganza's encounter with the witch and her direct personal contact with evil and its source, is of profound importance to the story and its meaning. But here we can mention only
one aspect of it. This is the curious fascination exercised upon Berganza by her story that he was originally a human baby, but was
changed into a puppy, and by her recounting of the prophecy that
he will regain human shape "when the proud are brought low and
the humble raised up" (310). It is curious that after all he has seen of
humankind, and suffered from them, he nevertheless hankers after
human form. It is even more curious that he appears inclined to
believe in his relationship to a witch, until Cipión dismisses both
story and prophecy as fraudulent nonsense. If Berganza's mind is so
unsettled by the thought of possibly becoming something other than
he is, of rising in status, on the word of a witch, what does this imply
for the merchants' and their sons' desires to be "better" than they
are? Or the desire of Pablos the Cheat to be "better" than he is? Are
all such ambitions, in Cervantes' view, the whisperings of the
Devil? One can put question after question in this way to the text of
this story and, by eroding trust in the storyteller ("it is impossible to
get along . . . without mutual trust and confidence"!), we could dis-
count entirely his vision of the world by refusing to accept his experience as it stands. Note that one can accept the possibility of his

experience without necessarily generalizing it. One could even say that Berganza's doggish experience among men is typical, without demanding that such experience be taken as typical *human* experience. What we cannot do is accept the dogs' experience and make it yield an ultimate truth about human life, and this is not because the particular dogs are unreliable but because such truth must be arrived at in view of the total work, and in order to achieve a total view a number of internal perspectives must be resolved.

One can soon come to suspect absurdity in one's own questions because, of course, Cervantes has so framed his story that we cannot expect to get answers. Each level of fiction abruptly shifts to a new one just as we are getting our balance in it and coming to feel some confidence in our perceptions. In particular, the story of the dogs is supposedly overheard by a delirious soldier in hospital. In the outer, "frame" story, the Licentiate Peralta refuses to believe in this dialogue. We know that dogs do not talk, so we feel a natural sympathy with his point of view. Yet, as he confesses, and as we would again have to agree, it is possible for us not to *believe in* talking dogs as a matter of experience, but still to *believe* talking dogs as a matter of fiction, that is as a rhetorical mode of truth-telling. New questions arise, of course. Does the dogs' conversation represent the mind of the ensign cleared of illusion? Or has he gone from credulity to cynicism? Is the *Dialogue* a kind of purging through dreams of his own desire to deceive and to be deluded? There is no easy answer to such questions, and I will not attempt to pursue them here. I have been concerned simply to make clear how far Cervantes has gone beyond anything that can be called characteristically picaresque in the *Dialogue*. Its content, the picture of a world of violence, alienation, and deception, is not greatly different from that of Lazarillo, Guzmán, or Pablos. The significance of that content is radically altered; in fact, the possibility of "picaresque" significance itself is made problematic by the originality of the formal structure to which it is adapted.

There are, among the narrative elements themselves some remnants of picaresque, but so transformed as to appear travestied. The first person narrator is not, as we might say of an unpleasant person, a "dog," but a real *dog*. (In our common speech, dogs are not often exemplary models, a fact which Berganza and Cipión conveniently overlook.) Lazarillo and Guzmán have mothers who are of rather easy virtue, and Pablos' is a reputed witch. Near the end of Berganza's narration we are told that he, too, may have a mother who was a witch. Like Lazarillo, he goes from master to master, and like Guzmán (or the later *Alonso Servant of Many Masters*) he has taken refuge in a more pious way of life. He even applies to himself a phrase used by Guzmán on more than one occasion—"I'm basically good" (*tengo buen natural* [237]) and if Guzmán recalls many years later the bits of Latin he picked up in the house of the cardinal, Berganza can also quote to Cipión the Latin that he learned from being in class at the Jesuit school!

But the principal differences between this novella and the picaresque novels we have discussed are to be summed up in what we observed at the beginning of this chapter with reference to Ginés de Pasamonte in *Don Quixote*. Berganza is not a sulf-sufficient narrator, and his story is not just a slice of raw experience. It only takes shape in dialogue; Cipión is as necessary to the *telling*, which is to say the significant ordering of the life, as Berganza himself. The individual self cannot see itself, much less know itself and reveal itself to us, in isolation. Berganza must have Cipión, just as Campuzano must have Peralta, and as Don Quixote must have Sancho Panza. Then again the whole of the *Dialogue* needs to be seen in its relation to the *Marriage*, and both in the context of a friendship renewed, because it is in this close-up view of the two men that we see trust and confidence restored, not in the retrospective panorama scanned by the dogs.[4] I think I have said enough to show that Cervantes' gesture to the recent novels was that of a brilliant putdown by way of adopting some of their basic mechanical parts. The *Dialogue of the Dogs* relegates the autobiography to a story within a story, and has a principal character dispute the truth of it. *Rinconete and Cortadillo*, in the words of a French critic, is a "novel in which the characters appear on the scene and vanish without any novelistic necessity controlling their entrances and exits."[5] Cervantes' pieces are open-ended in a more radical way than anything which preceded them. However, we must not close our eyes to another possibility, which is that diversity and creative conflict may be as much a part of this picaresque tradition as stability of forms and continuity of subject. Uncertainty about whether or not to call Cervantes' novellas "picaresque" derives from differing convictions about what are the essential qualities of a picaresque fiction.[6] This question must be left to chapter 8.

CHAPTER 6

From Espinel to Estebanillo González

I Vicente Espinel and Marcos de Obregón

VICENTE Espinel (1550–1624) was born in Ronda, in Andalusia and lived there for most of his first fifty years. He was ordained priest: his uncle had endowed a chaplaincy, and the priesthood seems to have offered him a secure profession rather than a spiritual vocation. Espinel could be called without offence a worldly man. He was a poet, one of the best of his day, and a great musician. He enjoyed company. He wrote long verses to patrons and friends which refer to his appearance and his ailments, but not to the state of his soul. After studying in Salmanca and traveling in various parts of Spain and Italy, he found Ronda a cramped place to which to return, although in *Marcos de Obregón* he praises the toughness that it breeds in its men. He had to be hauled back from Madrid under royal orders and the threat of severe penalties before he would attend to chaplaincy duties at the poor people's hospital. In 1599 he had the opportunity to escape to Madrid as organist and choirmaster, and there he spent the rest of his life among witty courtiers and the, quite literally, unnumbered writers who thronged Madrid in those years. He was an official censor of books, and had the reputation of being a sharp satirist.

Like so many other writers, he wrote only one novel, *Life of the Squire Marcos de Obregón* (*Vida del escudero Marcos de Obregón*, 1618), and it contains a quantity of recognizable autobiographical material. It is related, moreover, in the first person, and there are abundant journeys and misfortunes. The book was traditionally judged to be a picaresque work, but in recent years this judgment has been questioned, and the change is of interest. With this change of category taking place, we may suppose the novel to be at some boundary, and it can perhaps help us to perceive differences between picaresque and nonpicaresque.

92

Marcos' life story begins with his boyhood in Ronda and ends with his decision, when an old man, to abandon the world and live in solitude, the better to prepare for death. The course of his life has taken him to Italy, to captivity in Algiers, and into service with some titled persons of the Spanish nobility. Like Guzmán de Alfarache, he has been a student, he has come to a point in his life at which he has to make a break with the past, and his story is stuffed with commentaries, discussions, disquisitions, and expostulations with himself as he narrates. This is not a profound conversion, however: nor, on one level, is it a written story but an orally delivered one.

The book begins with the narrator as an elderly inmate of the charity hospital of Santa Catalina in Madrid. His mind goes back to the time when he was in service with a Doctor Sagredo as *escudero* or squire (attendant and chaperon to the doctor's wife), and this leads to the moment when, caught in a storm at a hermitage outside Madrid, he tells the hermit the story of his life. Thus the bulk of the narrative is a monologue whose content is recalled and repeated in the writing of the autobiography. The reason for writing the book is not to justify himself, but to provide some instruction balanced with entertainment, adapting the well-known formula of Horace. Compared to existing picaresque models, then, *Marcos de Obregón* lacks the peculiar relationship of the narrator with the reader, the act of writing is less completely motivated, and the means of telling is less plausible. The spoken narrative is broken into two parts, because when darkness falls Marcos spends the night in the hermitage and resumes his story next day. As a spoken memoir, later recalled to form the major part of a written one, its procedure is peculiar. But this is only one of a number of features which are strained or arbitrary. The hermit, for example, recognizes Marcos when they first meet; they were together in Seville and Italy and Flanders. Yet Marcos' narrative contains no recollection of any experiences which he shared with his host. On the other hand, the novel does contain much that is truly autobiographical: like Espinel, Marcos was a native of Ronda, spent time in Italy, had Espinel's gout and other physical ailments, and knew many of the people whom Espinel knew.

If we turn our attention to the motivation of the *Life*, we find that Marcos is not hungry for success or acceptance, and seldom even feels the itch of mischief. He is an honest man who stays honest, and does not blame the world for what he is. Even the occasional practi-

cal jokes are committed in self defense, with the exception of the
painful assault on his jailer in book 3, chapter 2. Consequently, this
is not a story of achievement whether told straight or ironically, and
there can be no question then of a plot so structured as to evaluate
that achievement through the medium of verbal and formal patterns. This is not to say that *Marcos de Obregón* is failed picaresque,
or that it lacks an intrinsic interest. Marcos is partly Espinel's alter
ego, partly invention, and there is a similar mingling of autobiography and romantic adventure in the plot.[1] What it tells us about
picaresque, I think, is that writers did not necessarily regard it as a
genre, whose integrity had to be preserved, but as a bundle of
possibilities, which could be taken apart and exploited separately.
Espinel is one writer who responded to the genre by experimenting
in his own way with autobiographical narrative, flashback, and an
episodic life taken as a cumulative experience. Other writers will try
to use other parts of picaresque as a point of departure: we shall
encounter stories of thwarted aspirations to social ascent, for example, and others which are just series of ingenious frauds. The success
(as distinct from the value) of *Lazarillo de Tormes* and *Guzmán de
Alfarache* was not to be seen in the repetition of total structure or
ideological message by later writers, but in the new imaginative (or
merely sensationalist) possibilities which they suggested.

The world of Espinel appears to be fundamentally good and
reasonable, and the well-intentioned person can make his way in it
without sacrificing integrity or suffering unusual humiliations. The
author was not exacerbated in his moral being, as Alemán was, or
sardonically intolerant like Quevedo, nor was he concerned to make
risky lunges against powerful social prejudices, as Lopez de Ubeda
did by means of his burlesques. Espinel was an agreeable socializer,
gregarious and entertaining, and though his fictional alter ego is
serious, even solemn, he finds the world manageable and rather to
his liking. "Instead of a psychological, spiritual, and social tension
between good and evil, he produced an agreeable enough, but
rather commonplace, balance that points directly to the neo-classical world of Lesage, on whose *Gil Blas* he exercised the greatest
single influence," writes Parker (55). "Neo-classical" is indeed an
appropriate epithet for Espinel, and it is surprising how often this
early seventeenth-century Spanish priest refers to God by such cir-
cumlocutions as the First Cause, or the Author of Life.

Marcos de Obregón is called the squire, in the title of the book. In terms of medieval knighthood, "squire" meant a servant who carried the weapons of the knight, waited upon him, and so on. Among the seventeenth-century urban aristocracy, however, it usually meant a retainer of mature years and dignified deportment who accompanied a woman when she went out alone, to shield her from unwanted attentions, open a way for her in crowded places, find her a seat, and perform similar services. It is an apt denomination for Marcos, a man of mature sense who guides others toward a more settled and serene control of themselves. In the earlier part of the book he helps Mergelina, the flighty wife of Doctor Sagredo, to escape from some embarrassing predicaments, until she eventually sees her own folly and changes her ways. Later, while he is in captivity in Algiers, a Moorish girl who is interested in becoming a Christian falls in love with him, although he is much older than she is. He loves her too, but painfully hides his feelings and gently tries to soothe and redirect her love, to make her see him as a second father. Much later, he meets these persons again, and is gratified to find that they have not deviated from the pattern of behavior that he set for them.

Marcos is as far from subversive as it is possible to be. He sees the risks and the injustices of life, but opposes his "noble breast" to them. He has a noble model of right conduct and a rational approach to difficult situations: exhibit patience, and look beneath the appearances. Humility is for him the greatest virtue, and dissatisfaction the seed of all destructive conflict.

The poor have pity on other poor people, but not on the rich. If only they could see truly how much more burdened the rich are by obligations and cares than the poor, they would certainly not exchange their lot for that of the rich man. Everyone tries to pull the rich man down, but nobody envies the poor, and yet their greatest comfort is slandering whomsoever is richer or better off than they are. (950b)

Recognize power and wealth, and respect their owners. Have patience and humility. Persevere in self-knowledge. On a few such axioms Marcos makes his way among the rocks and shoals of life. He is invited by a friend to visit the kitchen of a nobleman's house where perhaps he will find employment. The servants are slovenly and quarrelsome, fighting for precedence, careless about service. After reproaching some of them, and being answered with insolence, he withdraws from this bedlam and retires to his home and his "friends":

> Among them I found consolation for the enslavement I could see lying in wait for me, I assuaged my hunger with a piece of bread which I had kept wrapped in a napkin, and dieted upon a chapter in praise of fasting. Oh books! You faithful counselors, friends without flattery, prompters of the intelligence, teachers of the soul, tamers of the body, guides to a good life, and watchmen for a good death! . . . (954a–b)

Stoical self-knowledge and respect for authority in all its aspects (social, intellectual, religious, or as embodied in traditional wisdom) are a long way from the world of Lazarillo. And the consistency of outlook in the protagonist, who progresses from his early mistakes to a greater maturity and capability, is equally far from Guzmán. To conclude, in the words of Richard Bjornson, who has dedicated some excellent pages to this writer, "Marcos' version of reality actually constitutes a justification of the existing social order. Even the wearing of masks becomes acceptable if they are employed to cope with momentary aberrations from the social norm. . . . Operative on both psychological and social levels, the pattern of temporary defeat and ultimate victory reaffirms his belief in himself and in the natural justice of the world in which he is living"[2] The Picaresque Hero, pp. 80–81)

II Dr. Jerónimo de Alcalá Yáñez and his Alonso

Doctor Jerónimo de Alcalá Yáñez (1563–1632) lived most of his life in Segovia, following the career of medicine, as his father, grandfather, and great-grandfather had done, and as his two brothers also continued to do. He served the city of Segovia as salaried physician and surgeon to its poor. Also he was in the service of the Marqués de los Vélez, as his forbears had been. He is then an obvious example of the amateur status of the writer. Like other writers of his time he wrote both for the entertainment and for the improvement of his readers (Alemán wrote a Life of St. Antony of Padua in addition to his Guzmán). His first work was the Miracles of Our Lady of Fuencisla, Glories of her Temple, and Festivities in the City of Segovia on the Occasion of her Translation . . . in the Year 1613 (Milagros de Nuestra Señora de Fuencisla . . .) published in 1615. The last, published posthumously in 1632, was Truths for the

Life of a Christian (Verdades para la vida cristiana). With these pious writings Alcalá Yáñez courted the praise of the learned men of his community, but without success. This is not to say that he conceived his novel-writing as frivolous; like Alemán he also thought of his fiction as instructive though in a different way from his didactic works. Critical judgment has treated them in contrary ways, for whereas Alemán's novel has been faulted for its didactic digressions, Alcalá Yáñez' more solemn works were instantly attacked for their lack of seriousness.

When he published part 1 of *Alonso, Servant of Many Masters* (1624), Alcalá Yáñez was sixty-one years of age. His book is that of an aging provincial who had little, if any, contact with the literary world of Madrid, and who was not continually exercising himself in the craft of writing. Like everyone else, he wrote a few verses, but when he published part 2 of *Alonso* in 1626, there was no indication that he intended to write any more fiction.

The hero of the story is a boy who is adopted after his father's death, by his uncle, a stern miserly priest who beats him, and who also has a grim housekeeper. He runs away from home and joins a group of students who are on their way to Salamanca, where he undergoes the ordeal of spitting originally described by Pablos in *El Buscón.* These "merry" students spend their time stealing, vandalizing, and provoking fights. When they leave him stranded, Alonso joins a captain in the army. The company of soldiers cheats, loots, and terrorizes the countryside until the captain is killed in a battle with angry villagers. Alonso takes sanctuary in a church, and is employed as assistant by the sacristan, who is sloppy in his duties and earns the boy's continual reproaches. Eventually he is dismissed for not minding his own business. This, with variations, will be the pattern of the whole book.

In succession, Alonso serves a ridiculous gentleman with an ugly wife, a magistrate in Córdoba, a physician in Seville, and a widow in Valencia. He finds himself in prison after the widow manages to kill an intruder who killed her son and intended to rape her. Released, he goes back to Seville and finds a master who has just been appointed to a high police position in Mexico, so he emigrates. In Mexico he dabbles in commerce and makes a large fortune which is lost when a boat in which he has invested goes down on its way to China. He returns penniless to Spain where he joins a company of actors as master of the wardrobe, and plays a few small parts, until the company breaks up. Next, he joins a priest who takes him to a convent of nuns, and he becomes a lay brother. This convent is where he is telling his story to the prior's deputy, the *vicario*.

In part 2, published two years later, Alonso is asked by a priest from a parish near to where he has now become a hermit to continue his story. He begins by telling how he was dismissed from the convent because he interfered and gave unwanted advice. On the road from there he is seized and stripped of his clothing by gypsies. He gains their confidence and becomes a tinker and a practitioner of deceits to gain money, gypsy-style, in the neighboring towns. He runs away, and after adventures and periods as a servant in different parts of Spain and Portugal he takes ship for Barcelona, but the vessel is driven by storms onto the North African coast where the occupants are taken captive. By chance he is with the same company of actors as before. They are commanded to entertain their masters, so ill-advisedly they perform a play on the revolt of Granada which shows the Spanish crushing the Moors. Naturally their masters are offended and the actors are executed, but Alonso manages to save himself. The story ends when he is ransomed by Trinitarian missionaries and returns to Spain to live out a life of solitary expiation.

Alcalá Yáñez follows Espinel in presenting an autobiography in the form of a spoken narrative. Yáñez' interlocutors are given more to say, but the weaknesses are the same. First, each of the two interlocutors (the two are hardly distinguishable) is entirely passive during most of the narration. The few comments and queries serve merely as reminders that someone is there, listening to Alonso, and that Alonso is addressing him, not us. The second weakness is that the story is being spoken to someone within the fiction itself, whereas the great innovation of *Lazarillo* and *Guzmán* was that they were addressed to a person ("Your Honor"; the "Wise Reader," i.e., you, me) who is presumed to be *outside* the book. Since both Lazarillo and Guzmán write for a reader whose motive in reading they are unsure of, there is a continuous play of doubts and uncertainty between what he says and what he might have said, but which we shall never know. The reader outside the book greatly complicates the point of view because of this need of the I-narrator to adopt a posture, to assure himself of the unseen reader's benevolence, to make himself all-of-a-piece, to give his random life the consistency of fiction, just as he would if he were called to account for himself before a judge. Lázaro knows that "Your Honor" will judge him;

Guzmán forces the reader to judge him; Alonso merely satisfies a curiosity which has nothing judicial in it. The two successive interlocutors invite him to talk because he is there. Since we as readers no longer occupy the position of the person addressed, we are not involved in the process of the novel, by which the I-as-object becomes the I-as-subject, the narrated becomes the narrator. Finally, the oral autobiography of Alonso is incongruous because it is addressed to two persons, neither of whom shows any interest in writing it down. It ought to have dispersed and vanished in the air, so how did it become recorded in this solid book? Alcalá Yáñez has failed to account for the author and for the act of writing—a rather elementary concern when a first-person perspective is being adopted. The autobiographical mode, then, not only has lost the complexities that went with being confessional, but it has ceased to be fully functional because it has not absorbed the narrator as writer.

The sequence of events does not become a coherent, cumulative experience. In *Lazarillo* and *Guzmán* the sensation of the reader is like that of a spring coiling back on itself, because the end is not just the end, but it is what justifies the beginning. In *Alonso,* events simply follow one another. If the hero (for want of a duller word) goes to another city, it may be because he has to flee; but it could as well be because he is merely curious to see it, or because the susceptibilities of a local audience are being flattered. So the author lays a small bit of the action in Segovia and tells the story of the miracle of the Jewess Esther and the Virgin of Fuencisla. Each city visited is introduced with an encomiastic list of its virtues, its noble families, its fine buildings, and so on, in a fashion used by a number of fiction writers of that decade.[3] Some of these cities are clearly associated with the author's patrons.

Other deviations from the prototypical picaro may be noted. Alonso is born of a respectable family and in the very first chapter speaks of the evidence for believing he inherited "good blood" from his parents. Then again, his knavery is little more than boyish mischief. He is soon scandalized by the behavior of the students and attempts to persuade them to see the error of their ways. Traditional picaresque haunts do not attract him. He spends as little time as possible as an errand boy in Seville (I, 6) and his sojourn among the actors brings out no gifts for verbal illusion or for multiple identities (I, 9). We wonder, as we read, what ingenious or necessary act will cause Alonso to be transformed from the object of the narrative to the subject, but there is none, for he is the same garrulous, well-intentioned, right-thinking person that he always was, wagging the same admonitory finger through a lifetime of minor misfortunes.

Earlier picaros were proud of their adaptability, their ease in learning new tricks and trades, and Alonso is no exception in this. Each time that he has to look for a new master, he convinces a complete stranger that he is the very assistant or servant who is needed. "I don't have to be told twice what to do," he tells the gentleman in Lisbon (1306). This versatility exceeds credibility when, deciding to make the best of his captivity among the gypsies, he volunteers to learn the craft of metalworking. He is given a hammer and "in two days I could compete with any follower of Vulcan's trade" (1283). Later (and by this time he is middle-aged), a painter accepts him as apprentice—because he happens to need one, and Alonso is there. Indeed, the ease with which he finds employment is not merely notable, it is consistent, and suggests that the author is making his book the vehicle for a Samuel Smiles ideology of success through personal effort. In (I, 8), even the passive Vicario is surprised at the ease with which a well-dressed stranger is persuaded to take Alonso as a servant, and the latter replies that diligence is the mother of good fortune, and that he was never one for sitting around with his hands folded like some idlers he's known, who complain that they cannot find work . . . (1254). In short, his aspiration is to be a good servant and give satisfaction rather than to achieve independence or transform himself socially. His disappointment is not to be traced to a world that is hostile, and certainly not to any insufficiency in himself, but rather to the defects in his masters and companions. The novel is crammed full of maxims, exempla, anecdotes, fables, and little sermons with which he either regales the listening Vicario and priest, or had previously addressed to his master. More than once he is dismissed for his talking out of turn, and this is the only fault which, after all these years, he finds in himself. As Samuel Gili Gaya wrote, Alonso talks "like one who has much to teach and nothing to learn. All his actions are justified, and only those of others need justification."[4] He never looks back ironically at his former self. There is no gap between the picaro and the self-righteous narrator to be explained.

It does not seem to matter much that Alonso takes employment in a religious house at the moment when he does, or that he has to leave, except that he feels unjustly treated. But the most curious example of the lack of meditation on events, the failure to tie the inner and outer worlds, occurs near the end of part 2. The actors have been sentenced to death by their Muslim masters, but Alonso protests, and points out that he only played the prologue and a few extra parts. He gets his reprieve, but the others do not. They accordingly go to their deaths "offering their necks most willingly to the yoke of martyrdom, declaring that they would give their lives not once but many times over for the sake of the truth of the holy Gospel." The priest remarks that he might have been the holy martyr Alonso if he had gone with the others, to which Alonso replies, without irony, "I didn't deserve such a blessing; even in this my talkativeness was my undoing. If I had not spoken up and appealed for my companions, I would have enjoyed the same happy end as they" (1339). Apparently no questions linger in his mind after this, and he does not even say how he came to be a hermit and what wrongs, if any, he is expiating. Perhaps Alcalá Yáñez was influenced by the popularity of Lope de Vega's play on the legendary martyrdom of St. Genesius, *Lo fingido verdadero* (1618; reprinted twice under the title *El mejor representante* 1621, 1622).

Some of the more interesting parts of this book are those which point in the direction of descriptive realism, unlikely as that may seem. The horrors of traveling by mule wagon and on foot on flooded dirt roads, and the furious revolt of villagers against marauding soldiers are two examples. Unfortunately, they are also evidence that Alcalá Yáñez had not thought very deeply about what his autobiographical novel was meant to be.

III *Castillo Solórzano*

Alonso de Castillo Solórzano (1584–1648?) was a prolific writer of novels, plays, and poetry, particularly of novellas which he gathered into collections.[5] Usually these collections had a novelesque pretext: a gathering of people in a country house to entertain one another by telling stories each day, for example. Castillo spent most of his life serving in noblemen's houses, including that of the Marqués de los Vélez with whom Alcalá Yáñez was associated. He cultivated long novels as well as the shorter kind and in the picaresque he presented both male and female rogues. Thus he is discussed in this chapter, and again in that which we have devoted to "The Rogue Female" (chapter 7).

In one of his early collections of short fiction *Pleasant Evenings* (*Tardes entretenidas*, 1625) Castillo included his first exercise in picaresque: *The Proteus of Madrid* (*El Proteo de Madrid*).[6] The hero is a foundling, the son of a Galician serving girl, left on the doorstep of a middle-aged gentleman who brings him up. The child becomes mischievous and devises endless tricks and frauds. The story is designed to amuse the internal audience to whom it is recited orally. Narrative viewpoint is less important than an entertaining delivery in these circumstances. A moral is stated at the beginning by the story-teller: "The narrative I have prepared for you is the life of an impudent lad who, because he was not corrected in his childhood, was punished by justice, to his shame. I urge parents to correct and punish their children, and governors their subjects . . ." (151). This scarcely matters, nor does the fact that the story ends with the youth in the galleys, because this is now a conventional outcome. He does not share Guzmán's anguish, for the narrator informs us "I have heard that he is on his bench performing a thousand practical jokes and swindles on his companions, so that his name may redound to future ages . . ." (203). Castillo can make the convict's life sound like good clean fun.

His single long novel around the adventures of a male trickster is *The Adventures of Bachelor Trapaza* (1637). The name of the leading character *trapaza*, means "cheat" or "fraud," and the surnames of his parents were Trampa ("trap") and Tramoya ("trick"). From the first, then, we are given an indication of the author's joking style. This is the story of a sharp boy conceived out of wedlock (his father marries the mother on his deathbed after being mortally wounded by her father) like so many of Castillo's comic heroes and heroines. As a child he is mischievous and spends his time at school gambling and composing satirical verses. He goes to the University of Salamanca in the company of some rich students and fleeces them at cards. Having money, his impulse is to dress up as a nobleman, assume a false name, adopt the title "don," and try to marry a girl who has a noble pedigree. He does fall in love with a certain Doña Antonia María de Monroy, and she tolerates his attentions and his serenades until her real boyfriend Don Enrique returns from a visit. Then Trapaza is no longer welcome and, moreover, favored Enrique recognizes him and makes his imposture public. Later Trapaza, Vargas (his associate), and Estefanía (a maid) become a trio of tricksters and set out for Seville. The group breaks up when Trapaza

Teresa de Manzanares is from Galicia, and so is Dominga Pérez in *El Proteo de Madrid*) are figures of fun. The seduction of a peasant girl is told in a flippant style, in contrast to the melodrama which such an event becomes in an aristocratic setting. Such a novel is picaresque in certain outward aspects only; the socially determined character of such categories as the comic and the serious show that it is essentially conformist in a way that the earlier novels never were. If Trapaza wins at cards, he can dress well and allow the author to describe the world he enjoys describing, and delay the moment when his picaro has to lose at cards and so rejoin the lower class. There is some mild ridicule of such well-established targets as carters and their oaths, duennas, stingy lovers, and innkeepers.

The *Adventures of Bachelor Trapaza* ends with the, by now, conventional sentence to punishment in the galleys. In contrast with *Guzmán de Alfarache*, however, this is simply a convenient way of stopping the otherwise endless sequence of adventures. The fact of being a convict does not enter into the narrative nor, of course, into the experience of the protagonist. The narration is all in the third person, as we have noted, so the consciousness of the protagonist is not represented. The prologue contains some conventional moralizing: ". . . the debauched life of a swindler, written with the purpose that people will beware of such men. . . . The author begs you not to look to the outer husk but to the beneficial part within . . ." (1428). The ending hands out some small doses of remorse: doña María regrets her credulity, and Estefanía regrets having sent Trapaza to the galleys, "so sudden is a woman's anger based on jealousy, that it is compared to gunpowder, quick to explode" (1527). A *Second Part* is promised, which turns out to be *The Seville Wildcat (La garduña de Sevilla)*, the life of Trapaza's daughter. This is examined below in chapter 7.

IV   Life and Deeds of Estebanillo González

The full title of this book, as it appeared on the title page of the first edition in 1646 is: *Life and Deeds of Estebanillo González, a Man of Merry Humor, Written by Himself (La vida y Hechos de Estebanillo González, hombre de buen humor. Compuesto por el mismo)*. The royal copyright *(privilegio)* names Estebanillo González as the sole grantee, and the certificate *(aprobación)* written by the ecclesiastical censor (every book published in the Spanish territories carried one) also refers to him as the author. Here, then, appears to be an anomaly, for a work which has traditionally held a place in the history of the novel is seemingly not a novel but a memoir. But the uncertainty is increased by the fact that we know nothing about Estebanillo González, and his name comes to us only in this book. Is this a real autobiography, we may ask, written by a man who would otherwise never have been known, or is it a novel written pseudonymously with the author adopting the name of his protagonist? Or is there some other answer? The book itself is written in the first person, but of course we may expect that in a picaresque novel. There is a real dilemma: how to read this book? As fact or as fiction? Is it life or invention? Experience or imagination?[9] Such puzzling and ill-defined works as this remind us that literary genres are not entirely capricious, and questions of genre are not idle, since they play an important part in how we read literature. From a literary point of view, Don Quixote's madness is the consequence of just such a generic confusion: what others took for fiction he took for fact. The question, What kind of book is this? is seldom merely naive or pedantic.

Estebanillo the narrator calls himself a "Spanish-Italian transplant" because he was born in Galicia and baptized in Rome (1726). Ambiguities of this sort continually fuel his punning style. His father was a painter—which allows him to exploit the pun *pintar* "to paint" and "to gamble at cards" (1727). We have seen how, from *Lazarillo* on,/it has been customary to address a prologue to the reader. Estebanillo González begins his, "Dear—or cheap—reader, or whoever you may be, if you like to pry into other people's lives and come to read mine, my name is Estebanillo González, the cream of hoodlums" (1723). So far the approach is familiar and reminds the reader of *Pícara Justina*, or *El Buscón*. But there are some curious twists. Estebanillo's father was an embarrassment, not because he was a thief or because he had dubious lineage, but because, on the contrary, he was an *hidalgo*, a pure-blooded gentleman. If a gentleman was born poor, he was likely to remain so, because such a person could lose his standing if he attempted to make a living in any way which was considered inappropriate. There is some slight insinuation against the integrity of his mother who died "of a craving for mushrooms while she was pregnant by my father, so she said," (1727) but his pretty sisters sit at home and do embroidery, as models of propriety. Estebanillo is not a hungry status-seeker rejecting an ignominious family and looking for an entry into the world of respectability at whatever cost.

He grows up in Rome, becomes a notorious prankster among the students, and is apprenticed by his father to a barber. One day his master steps out of the shop and Estebanillo is left with the customer, a macho hoodlum who has come to have his huge curled and pointed mustachios dressed to the desired pitch of aggressive flamboyance. Estebanillo will not admit that he is not qualified, so he plunges a red-hot iron into the bushy face. He has to flee, waving the iron with half a pointed mustache'stuck on the end, and leaving the proud facade a smoking ruin. The scene is brilliant slapstick comedy, but not typically picaresque. As an occasion for leaving home it has no connection with family poverty, or personal ambition, or desire to prove one's worth. Rather, the boy makes himself the object of laughter by his incompetence. There are other barbering mishaps in a later chapter when he returns to Rome for a second chance, when the elaborate descriptions of botching with blunt razors through billowing suds, and ears snipped in a bravura of scissor work foreshadow the narrator's later profession as court jester.

Estebanillo's career is a variegated one. He serves in the army several times, deserts, sells pins, trinkets, and cosmetics, and is sentenced to death for killing a man in a fight, but has his sentence commuted. At times he lives by gambling and swindling, at others he survives day by day as a hired laborer. This much he has in common with recognizable picaros, that he does not join the army for any selfless, patriotic motives. He is either attracted by a glamorous officer and his line of talk, or he sees the opportunity to move to Italy, or he is down on his luck. On joining a company of French soldiers (chapter 5) he comments that he would have served the Turk in order to escape hunger. The nominal sense of honor which even the most cynical picaro retains in some form is entirely absent here. When Estebanillo kills a man, we are told offhandedly that it was over an accusation of "lying through the teeth," but he does not say who accused whom. Then, before we know it, the other man is dead: "my stab put him on his back because, not looking where I was, he got on the edge of my sword. He was killed by his own great arrogance, not by my great indifference" (1769). The episode is casual, perfunctory, empty of any residue of self-esteem.

The event seems to take its own absurd course, indifferent to personal evaluation. The *lance de honor*—affair of honor—is reduced to a mechanical tic in which it is no longer important even to know who was aggrieved, and for what cause. Later an even more ridiculous duel takes place (chapter 7); he and his opponent are both drunk and stagger about lashing the air with their swords at a safe distance from each other. The only person who gets hurt is one of the seconds.

There is no picaro in the earlier literature who would fail to protect his sense of personal worth if it were challenged, or who would not at least attempt to cover his shame from public scrutiny. Estebanillo, as we have seen, is not moved by such scruples, nor is he responsive to the collective form of honor, namely, patriotic feeling. No earlier picaro ever changes allegiance so easily, deserts so frequently, and is so disinclined to denounce the enemies of his king and his faith. In chapter 6 he is with the Spanish army marching from Flanders into Germany. It is the year 1634, during the Thirty Years' War, and long ago he decided that fighting was to be avoided and that he could not only live but live well as an army cook. Nevertheless, he finds himself caught in the engagement, and his account of it deserves quotation:

Dismayed at the event and terrified at hearing the thunder of the cruel cannon and seeing the lightning of the gunpowder and feeling the shot go streaking past, thinking that all Sweden was coming against me, and that I would lose an ear at the very least . . . I retired to an abandoned ditch near our army. This had become a refuge for the carcass of a nag with its legs splayed and its face up; no doubt it was counting the stars. Seeing that the musket fire was getting heavier, the drums beating, and the trumpets echoing, I got right close to it, stretched on the ground but with my face turned away because of the stench, so that the two of us looked like a plucked Imperial eagle. And since I still didn't seem to be as safe as I would like, and the enemy was master of the field, I threw the skinny steed on top of me like a quilt. . . .

Returning to camp when the action has moved away, he buries himself in the hayloft and pretends to be wounded. When it is safe he goes out and draws his sword "to give it some air. Standing a half league from both camps I put my hat in my left hand like a buckler and with my feet firmly planted I started yelling over and over: 'For St. James, St. James! Forward Spain, at them, at them! Forward, forward!' " He decides, now that the enemy are routed, to perform some act of courage. After making "a hundred thousand signs of the cross, arms trembling and legs like quicksilver" he comes upon a glade which is full of Swedish dead and begins furiously to attack the corpses, "slashing guts, opening bellies and slicing gullets; I'm not the first to wait till after the storm, or to stick a brave lance into a dead Moor. I wrought such great havoc that I paused to consider that no man is more cruel than a chicken which finds itself at an advantage or more brave than an honest man when he fights with cause." One of the bodies is not yet dead and lets out a groan: "It seemed to me that it was about to rise up and take complete vengeance so, not having the courage to pull the sword out from where I had run him through, I reckoned the better part of valor was to leave it with him and I turned my back and fled at top speed and didn't stop until I came to where our baggage train was. . . ." His commanding officer who has been mortally wounded, angrily asks him where he has been and why he did not carry out orders. Estebanillo's reply is " 'So as not to be as you are now. It's true I am soldier and cook, but I do my soldiering in the kitchen and cook as I can. . . . A soldier can't be in two places or serve two masters. . . .' They took him into the town where he gave up the ghost, because he wasn't as smart as I was."

I have quoted this episode at some length because it is probably the best example of what makes this book unlike any picaresque novel. The "marginality" by which so many commentators have characterized the picaro is now seen to be only relative, his inversion of values limited and provisional, in comparison with Estebanillo González'. Lazarillo claims some part of the glory of the victories of Charles V, and there is no doubt what Guzmán's choice would be if he had to choose between hunger and serving the Turk. Alonso praises (and says he envies) the "martyrdom" of the actors in Algiers. Cervantes never let us forget his participation in the naval Battle of Lepanto, the "most glorious occasion that past or present centuries have seen, nor future ones will ever see." One could hardly imagine, from Estebanillo's grotesque and ghastly description, that this is an equally "glorious" occasion: the battle of Nördlingen when the Spanish and Imperial forces destroyed the Swedish army. Estebanillo has not forgotten the obligatory words of eulogy, but they are curiously detached from the event, coming as they do in the following chapter when Estebanillo has resumed his more detached narrative style.

This *Life* does not have an imposed narrative structure, but is shapeless and indeterminate. The interest is in the variety of events and actions and in the narrator, a man who is committed to nothing but his own survival. Whatever he gains he loses because he gambles or is drunk. There is a rich social content, since the restless wandering boy rises to be a court buffoon who is even entrusted with diplomatic messages between Vienna, Warsaw, Brussels, Rome, and Madrid. As a jester, of course, he has to surrender all dignity, to flatter shamelessly, to share the status of a pet animal: well fed, threatened, beaten, rewarded, but always looking on at this world of artifice, ceremony, and honor like Tolstoy's horse, estranged and with an unsparing literalness. There is a moment of terror when his patron the Cardinal Infante dies, and he is completely alone, and no one wants to know him (chapter 9). Such a moment helps to explain, though not in our eyes to excuse, the painful anti-Jewish practical jokes. Estebanillo could not fail to exploit the satisfaction of finding people whose social respect was less than his own, or resist the temptation to unload the burden of self-mockery onto another scapegoat, a universally available one.

This book has provoked the most diverse responses. Juan Goytisolo[10] sees in it the positive act of stripping away façades with a "devastating sincerity" (21). "By restoring cowardice and baseness as necessary parts of human life, Estebanillo does us all a service" (26). For A. A. Parker, on the other hand, "It is true that at times it is genuinely funny . . . but on the whole it leaves a very unpleasant taste in the mouth. . . . It is a completely heartless book; there is nothing, not even his own soul that he can take seriously."[11]

V   *Antonio Enríquez Gomez*, Life of Don Gregorio Guadaña

This curious piece is part of a longer work, *The Age of Pythagoras* (*El siglo pitagórico*, *1648*), by a writer who because of his Jewish ancestry spent a large part of his life abroad to escape persecution. He also wrote interesting plays, poetry, and philosophical works. His novel is really a satirical fantasy based on the idea, attributed to the philosopher Pythagoras, of metempsychosis, or transmigration of souls. The *Siglo Pitagórico* takes the form of a series of reincarnations—miser, informer, demimondaine, royal favorite, religious hypocrite, new rich, among others. The story of Don Gregorio Guadaña is the last of the series. Rather than a picaresque narrative it is part of a larger plan of witty satirical assaults on recognizable social types already profiled in Quevedo's *Visions (Los Sueños)* and *The Limping Devil (El diablo cojuelo)* of Luis Vélez de Guevara. The protagonist's father is a doctor and his mother a midwife, and his extended family includes a pharmacist, a surgeon, a dentist, a nurse who specializes in enemas, a tutor to young girls who trains them in the oldest profession, an alchemist, a quack healer, and a few others. All of them are made the object of witty and vigorous satire. Gregorio leaves Seville to go to Salamanca to pursue a doctorate in law, but his adventures with fellow travelers (a judge, a notary, a constable, a lawyer, and a coach load of other targets for satire, such as braggart soldier, platitudinous priest, flighty girl and her calculating aunt) take him to Madrid where he becomes further embroiled in intrigues, some high-spirited, some desperate. The densely woven verbal wit and the comic ingenuity are unmatched by any writer except Quevedo. This work has been called a "witty and demonic pantomime";[12] for brilliantly irreverent critical intelligence one can only compare Enríquez Gómez with Valle-Inclán. His work was published in Rouen, France, in 1644, and it is curious to note that it was in that city that Estebanillo González practiced a swindle on Spanish-speaking Jews by posing as one himself (*Estebanillo González*, chapter 5).

Enríquez Gómez appears to be closer to the French adaptations of picaresque than to the Spanish originals. Charles Sorel's *Histoire comique de Francion* (1623, 1626, 1633) had taken French fiction away from the improbably idealized romances toward a more faithful representation of contemporary society. That society was explored critically, but by well-born heroes who, if they practice tricks, deceptions, and intrigue, do so in order to expose the deceits, falsehood, and hypocrisy of society. This satiric comedy of manners enabled the protagonist to retain the status of hero while he exposed the corrupters and imposters; he was not only the center of attention in the story, but the protector of society. When Sieur de la Geneste turned Quevedo's Pablos *El Buscón* into *L'aventurier Buscon* (1633), he did more than translate it. He transformed Quevedo's low-born upstart, condemned to frustration, into a hero who was superior in qualities of character to those around him. He was depicted as gallant and pleasure-loving, a sort of laughing cavalier who fully deserved to reach his happy end. This cultivation of a literary hero who exposes social shams from on the same social level as his influential adversaries, and from a higher moral level, has left its mark on Enríquez Gómez' Gregorio Guadăna. The protagonist is more of an observer than actor. His involvement is mostly confined to that of innocent bystander who is swept into the events, or satirical commentator on the persons with whom he shares the long journey by coach to Madrid.

VI   *Gregorio González*, El guitón Honofre

This work is mentioned last because, although it is dated 1604, there is no evidence that it was ever published. It recounts the origins and early adventures of Honofre (or Onofre) who is left an orphan and brought up by a widower in the company of his own son. The boy's natural parents were peasants, and there is nothing dishonorable either in their profession or their family connections, and this is true also of his adoptive family. There is therefore no inner motivation for him to reject his past in order to make good. The hero's youth is spent amid the beatings of a stepmother, privations in the house of a sacristan, the self-flagellations of an excessively devout student at Salamanca, and in inns with mule drivers; that is to say, in the established milieu for small deceits and trickery. Honofre is called a vagabond *(guitón)*, but he is no greater a wanderer than Lazarillo and far less so than Guzmán and others. There is no interest in the protagonist and his fate, and the story is a string of youthful pranks and practical jokes and acts of petty revenge. There are some sententious reflections and pious ruminating which waver between the genuine and the cynical. As an example of the latter, when Honofre has stolen the offerings from church, he is able to get his cloak out of pawn and comments: "Such is God's generosity that when he gives he is not content merely to give what is needful but anticipates our future wants" (197). After playing practical jokes on some Jesuits and swindling by means of forged letters, he enters a Dominican monastery in bad faith. The end promises a second part which will tell of his abandoning the religious life.

This novel by an unknown, once only writer (González was apparently an estate manager in the upper Ebro valley) is interesting for the fact that it turns Guzmán's conversion on its head. It gives further evidence for our contention that writers did not find authority in any specific picaresque model, but it remains within the field of the abundant literature of pranks and ingenious practical jokes which proliferated in the sixteenth and seventeenth centuries.

CHAPTER 7

The Pícara: *The Rogue Female*

MORE than one hundred years before the publication of *Moll
Flanders* by Daniel Defoe in 1722, the nonheroic,
nonidealized female protagonist had emerged in Spanish fiction. *La
pícara Justina* appeared in 1605, the year after part 2 of Aleman's
Guzmán de Alfarache. Thus variations on the picaro are emerging
swiftly, and each time with very pronounced originality. The female
protagonist, by the mere fact of being female, imposed new roles
and therefore changes of design upon the novel from the start. In
these novels there are no little girls put out to serve masters, as
Lazarillo is put out by his mother. Then again, young girls do not
leave home to seek a fortune on foot, as Guzmán does. Girls did not
go to the universities or join the army or walk the streets looking for
regular employment. All of these acts which obviously may be performed by the young male, are just as obviously impossible for the
young female of the 1600s, and so the novel which has a female protagonist will necessarily be different in shape and detail from that
which is dominated by a picaro. Whether or not the novel of the
pícara can remain recognizably a branch of that of the picaro is a
question which will interest us as we attempt to follow these new
developments.

I *López de Úbeda*, La pícara Justina

Licensed in 1604, this strange book was published the following
year in Medina del Campo. The author, Francisco López de Úbeda,
was a physician who appears to have been closely associated with
the court of King Philip III. He dedicated it to Don Rogrigo Calderón, the favorite of the king's minister. Unlike the earlier novels, in
which a clearly discernible plot is identical with the protagonist's life
as he shapes it in retrospect, this one is fragmentary. The narrator,
who following tradition is the protagonist herself, begins with a

113

lengthy introduction which consists of three chapters. In the first she addresses her pen which, as she begins to write, has a hair on it and this, of course, spoils the writing. The chapter is a seemingly endless series of puns on all the possible senses of the word *pelo* ("hair"), allusions to its remotest connotations, proverbial uses, and so on. The phrase "no tener pelos en la lengua" means to be free with one's tongue, and this is indeed applicable to her, since the whole book, not merely this chapter, is as A. A. Parker has said, "a riot of verbosity."[1] She alludes at length to the loss of hair which contemporary readers would immediately recognize as a symptom of syphilis. She also quarrels with the hairs which, as they fall from her head, leave a mark on her too-tender skin. The ravages of sex and of age, in falling hair and lines on the face, are but two of the many personal traits that Justina reveals by means of this nearly chaotic stream of associations which the word *pelo* starts up. As a result, she accuses the hair on her pen of causing her to reveal what she did not intend.

This feminine preoccupation with age and appearance is consistent with the author's declaration of purpose in his "Prologue to the Reader" ("Prólogo al Lector"). There he laments the quantity of profane literature which is to be found everywhere. People go to watch plays which are full of bad examples, and nobody nowadays reads edifying books, such as saints' lives. If he were to write the kind of book which ought to be written, no one would buy it, so he compromises by telling this story of "virtuous entertainment" *(honesto entretenimiento)* about a frivolous woman and her varieties. In fact, the doings of his "heroine" are extraordinarily mild, and anyone who reads the book on the proviso of this prologue with its "loose woman," its hints of sensuality, and Justina's talk of her fallen hair, will be disappointed. The story is a series of small incidents overlaid with an unquenchable flow of gossip and wordplay. The only sexually motivated incident is the abduction of Justina by a group of students, against whom she defends her virtue with great vigor, finally making them all look foolish. The fact that she is a woman does serve as a bait in working her swindles, of course, and this is characteristic of female rogue stories, as might be expected.

Although the action is slight, this is not a short work. It is divided into four books, and in length it falls between that of part 1 and part 2 of *Guzmán de Alfarache.* The typology of the hero insofar as we can establish one for Lazarillo, Guzmán, and Pablos, is not very closely adhered to. Justina's parents keep an inn, which inevitably means that they are light-fingered, that they overcharge, give their guests' horses short measure, post the tariff high up in a dark corner, and so on. Justina herself is well read, because a visitor once left a collection of books at the inn, and she read them all. She is descended from a long line of performers, who had the gift of the gab, and on her mother's side, in particular, they were of merry trades ("oficios alegres"): barber, mask-maker, tamborine maker. This last died while he was making a merry noise playing the bagpipes, when a man who had a grudge against him punched the chanter down his throat, with a quantity of his teeth. It could not be removed until a friend, a tavernkeeper, "with a great heave got it out of his body, as if getting a bagpipe out of the man's body were no different from pulling a funnel out of a wineskin dressed with pitch. Also, like the friend he was, he consented to be the executioner in this extremity. In short, with that tug the bagpipe came forth, and with it there flew away the leaping, hustling, prancing, dancing, jigging little soul, just like quicksilver. He died at his trade, and his trade died in him because there was no tamborine maker to take his place in all the region of Malpartida" (ed. Valbuena Prat. p. 736). This flippant way with injury, death, and disaster—the nearer the relative, the more lighthearted the style—is characteristic of this book and puts it closer in manner to Quevedo than to the earlier writers.

If Justina's parents are not model citizens, they are not as criminal or as cynical as others in picaresque literature. Their delinquency is of the petty kind taken for granted in members of their profession. But, as we have just seen, Justina goes far beyond what earlier picaros have done in the narration of their personal history. She is not content to inform the reader of her parents, but goes back through the four previous generations. Instead of following the established model, then, she tells a story which is exorbitantly stretched out in one direction, but anticlimactic in another. This is characteristic of much of the book: what is said is simply not to be measured on the same scale with what is done. Observe the following passage (book 1, chapter 3) which again presents a death, this time the death of Justina's mother. A pork butcher has left a string of sausages mounted on the spit over the fire in the inn. Justina tells how her mother, acting the part of an officer of the law, ordered the sausages to dismount, with their companions, the legs of lamb. They refuse and appeal to their absent master, and this burlesque of a police interrogation leads to an "arrest" in which the majority of the sausages are consigned to the prison of her stomach. When the butcher unexpectedly comes to rescue his "men," she hastily stuffs the rest of them into her mouth, where they are packed so tight that they can neither go forward nor retreat.

The butcher demanded an explanation on behalf of himself and his servants, but there was no answer at that door, which was jammed with sausage. And the best part of it was that besides having her throat stuffed, there was a length of sausage sticking out of her mouth so that some said she looked like a dragon in a coat of arms, with its tongue out, others said she was like a woman who had been hanged, to some she resembled a wineskin with its spigot, and to others a windpipe with a loose end, to others a newborn monster with its cord not yet cut; to some she seemed to be a conjurer with festoons coming from his mouth, and to others a snake in the entrance to a burrow. But to the butcher, who was smarting, she appeared as an ambush full of enemies, a den of thieves, and in short, the tomb of his sausages.

The bystanders try to remove the sausage with the spit and she finally dies of a fit and leaves Justina surprised that her soul could escape so easily through her crammed gullet. The witticisms continue for a while yet, over the laying out of the body and the burial.

In a book of this nature it is useless to look for psychological insight, human relations, significant plot. It would be easy to conclude that López de Úbeda was merely a garrulous writer taking advantage of the recent fashion for fictional autobiography and who relied heavily on verbal clowning to get him through. Of course, his readers would have been able to see how much he was fooling with earlier fictional motifs and situations. The picaros tell of their parents, so Justina goes back four generations. Whereas a picaro's parents are thieves or swindlers and variously immoral, Justina's are trivial cheats. All of her own acts are insignificant in themselves, and instead of being organized within the experience of a life, they are carried forward by a relentless and inspired frivolity, and carried in other directions by random associations, allusions, and puns. The life has no meaningful structure as plot, such as *Lazarillo de Tormes* and *Guzmán de Alfarache* lead the reader to expect. Justina is as she is from the first, and not as the result of a process of socialization by others. Another significant motif in the preceding novels, and in Quevedo's *Buscón*, is the initiation into society, which falls into two parts: a recognition, by means of some painful lesson, that he is not the equal of those around him, followed some time later by the demonstration that he has mastered the art of survival by his wits. So Lázaro is humiliated by the blind man at the stone bull, and he later reverses the relationship at the stone post. Pablos, *el Buscón* is several times pitched into or covered in excrement before he asserts himself as equal in knavery with everyone else. This motif is also absent from *La pícara Justina*. Rather than plot, one might speak of antiplot, in which each adventure is announced with great fanfare by the narrator, only to reveal itself as a small cheat, feeble misadventure, or the elaborate setting for a verbal squib. Even before picaresque has attained the status of a genre, it appears to be the object of vigorous parody.

Richard Bjornson, who sees two kinds of picaro, those who are born picaros and those who are molded by society, places Justina in the former class, along with Quevedo's Pablos. Quevedo and López de Úbeda, he writes, "portray similar characters in terms of inherently corrupt natures." Because they are both unworthy, and because they both aspire to move beyond the circumstances of their birth, they will both have their aspirations "a priori condemned as hypocritical and pretentious."[2] While this judgment is true enough of *El Buscón,* I would question its appropriateness for *La pícara Justina.* What does unite these two works is their respective authors' game of travesty with *Lazarillo de Tormes* and *Guzmán de Alfarache.* Each of them, though using different means, aims to show up the earlier works as mechanical in structure, and Guzmán in particular as overly charged with solemn moralizing. As Marcel Bataillon pointed out, we find cultivated here in *La pícara Justina* the new concept of *la picaresca:* a picaresque way of life.[3] The verses in praise of that life, *La vida del pícaro (The Rogue's Life,* ca. 1600), celebrate a joy in freedom, an almost evangelical "take no thought for the morrow" and "lay not up for yourselves treasures upon earth," so rich is the poor man's life made to seem. Of course, the poem is goliardic rather than evangelical, and it celebrates student poverty rather than real beggary or any spiritual benefits. We find this attitude again in Cervantes' story *La ilustre fregona (The Illustrious Kitchen Maid),* when a noble youth, Diego de Carriazo, runs away from home to the picaresque haunts for no other reason than his own high spirits: "no ill-treatment by his parents forced him into it, but only his pleasure and caprice".[4] Ironically, perhaps, Guzmán himself had joined in this chorus of praise with a eulogy of the beggar's life as one of "buen humor," merry and free from cares.[5] A long chapter in *La pícara Justina* (II, i, 1) is given to just such praise of singing, dancing, laughing, talking, and all kinds of merriment.

The researches of Bataillon also went a long way toward showing that *La pícara Justina* is by no means the insipid attempt to write a picaresque novel by an incompetent author, which earlier and puzzled readers had supposed it to be. The book is full of "in" jokes, according to Bataillon, and many of the ridiculous figures in it would have been recognizable as real people. The author may have been a converso; at any rate his book mockingly levels absence of lineage against the snobs and the power elite, and the prevailing obsession with "purity of blood." That part of the book which takes place in León can be explained by the recent (1601) visit of the royal court to that city. León, a northern city, capital of the early Christian kingdom of that name, center of refuge for Christians and of the counterattack against the Moors, was for all these reasons a symbol of Old Christian pride in ancestry. The episodes in this section of the book may be seen, then, as part of López de Úbeda's assault on the manifestations of this pride and the exclusiveness that went with it. There are jokes about family trees, the vast quantities of paper spent in proving one's descent, and even a kind of surrealistic transcription of inquisitorial investigations into family history.[6] Not everyone, obviously, accepted the humiliating statutes which excluded descendants of Jews from privileges and positions of power, or shared the obsession with honor found among rural Old Christians and upward-bound nouveaux riches alike. López de Úbeda boldly, and with a seemingly inexhaustible, vigorous, and sardonic verbal wit and fantasy, flayed these absurdities within view of the court itself. The Inquisition did not touch his book, and Rodrigo Calderón, the future royal favorite, was his patron. All of this indicates that the "converso mind" is not as monochrome as it is often represented, that converso writers did not all use subterfuges, conscious or unconscious, for expressing their anxiety in an intolerant society. López de Úbeda, like the famous Doctor Villalobos, spoke out by means of forceful ridicule. He must, obviously, have had listeners and readers. His art is the art of the buffoon, and he appears to have been a court joker as well as physician, enjoying a certain immunity for his acid comments by virtue of his position and his professional expertise, as well as his ironic self-deprecation. These are some of the qualities which we shall encounter again in the *Life of Estebanillo González*. His book would have been read as burlesque rather than as novel, as a sort of vaudeville script written for an attentive and sharp-witted audience. It has suffered the fate of all such literature that is relevant to its moment and to a particular public: it is almost meaningless to another audience and another time without the aid of an interpreter.

II   Salas Barbadillo, *Elena, Daughter of Celestina*

This novel (*La hija de Celestina*, 1612; longer version retitled *La ingeniosa Elena*, 1614) was clearly intended, by means of its title, to cash in on the success of one of Spain's great literary masterpieces, *La Celestina* by Fernando de Rojas. Rojas wrote a story of passionate love which came to an unhappy end with Calisto's fall to his death, and Melibea's suicide. But the average reader remembered most vividly the impressive figure of the old bawd who arranged their meeting, and although she, too, died in Rojas' work, she or her spirit lived on in a number of imitations and continuations in the sixteenth century, and Celestina-like figures appear frequently. Elena, the heroine (or antiheroine) of Salas Barbadillo's novel is not a daughter of the original Celestina, but her mother did have some of the same accomplishments in procuring and witchcraft, so Celestina became her proud nickname. The life story of Elena is comparatively short, and the narrated events occupy a small span of time. She is a confidence trickster, and the book relates the frauds which she achieves with Montúfar, her accomplice and paramour. First, she defrauds an old nobleman by convincing him that she was raped by his nephew, who is about to make a dazzling marriage. Elena has based her accusation on accurate information about the young man, and acts her distress (with her supporting cast of Montúfar, lady companion, and servants) so well that she gets her compensation, and they flee dressed as pilgrims. Next, after some traveling by road, they establish themselves in Seville as a saintly brother and sister who are engaged in all manner of charitable good works. Their holy poverty impresses the wealthy and influential people of the city, and they amass an enormous fortune from the alms they collect, and live in luxury behind the humble façade of their cabin. They are denounced by a servant who has a grudge against them but escape the city justices, although their servants pay the penalty. Moving to Madrid, Elena and Montúfar marry and he helps to increase their capital by introducing rich lovers to his wife. This lasts until he becomes angry that she is wasting her charms on an idle (and profitless) youth and has thereby lost a wealthy patron. He beats her, she takes vengeance by poisoning him; when he realizes this he attacks her, and her lover comes out of hiding and kills him. Elena and the young lover are executed. There have been some earlier (chapters 5–7) separations and unlikely reconciliations (after Montúfar had tied Elena and her woman companion to a tree in a forest and robbed, flogged, and insulted them!). Thus, we are meant to find the ending plausible, and to reflect that accomplices in crime are unstable partners (chapter 7).

The reader is asked to believe in the moral edification to be got from this. Vice is punished, indeed (when the author needs to put an end to his story), but there is no virtue to be rewarded; in fact, the virtuous donors in Seville are absurdly bamboozled, and their piety looks like stupidity. The author's attitude is ambiguous: violent punishments and melodramatic reversals, condemnations of Elena as a "base whore" (chapter 4; 904b), alternate with admiration for her ingenuity and for her beauty, and a sentimental indulgence because men's hearts (and their wits) dissolve when they look at her beautiful face. When Elena and her accomplice are denounced to the officers of justice in Seville, we are told that this was caused by the wrath of Heaven which, "unable to allow such wickedness to continue, drew aside the curtain of their hypocrisy, so their vices were stripped naked" (915a). Nevertheless, the pair escape with their fortune, so Heaven is left holding the curtain.

This novel is not told in the first person by the protagonist. She has been executed, and we are not told the status of the narrator or on what authority he narrates his story. Edwin B. Place saw this as an innovation, and likewise Salas' combining of picaresque low style with elements of the so-called *novela cortesana*.[7] *Novela cortesana* is the name conventionally given to the seventeenth-century fashionable stories of adventure. Upper-class characters are involved in plots of love and jealousy and sexual intrigue in expensive surroundings, well-known aristocratic names are used, and the tears, exclamations, sudden reversals of fortune, and final vindication of respectability all reveal this literature's similarity to Victorian melodrama. Unlike *Lazarillo de Tormes* and the other earlier picaresque novels, *Elena* begins not at the beginning of her life, but in the middle. We encounter the heroine in the street, making her entry into the city. Not until chapter 3 does she recount to her accomplice (and to us) the story of her life up to that point, when Salas invents a sleepless night for this purpose. This is nothing other than the age-old narrative formula for epic and romance, brought back into the picaresque novel. And it was the picaresque, in the example of *Lazarillo de Tormes*, which first symbolically renounced romance by beginning at the beginning and adopting the first-person narration. With first-person narration, the complex structure of interlocking episodes and hidden identities, of "While A is searching for B, he meets C who begins to tell his story, but is interrupted by the desperate cries of D who is bound to a tree . . . ," becomes both more difficult to manage and less plausible. An I-narrator, who addresses the reader directly, establishes a closer relationship with him and demands to be believed. The other side of the contract between the narrator and the reader is that the narrator must be believable. And since there is no independent teller to set the scene, the tone, the level of probability, and so on, the narrator and the reader must get along as best they can. Which means, in practice, that the narrator sets things moving by assuming more of a shared world between himself and the reader.

Salas Barbadillo's *Elena* is contemporary in setting, but reverts to romance in aspects of its structure. In addition to the third-person narration, the commencement at the middle, and the retrieval of the past at a later time, we may note that although the activities of our leading lady and her accomplices are not exactly the stuff of heroic romance, their ambitions and their pecuniary success enable them to operate at a social level which may have been above that of many of their readers. Then there are the disappearances and reappearances which the *novela cortesana* shared with the tradition of romance, and the sudden, inexplicable changes of sentiment. For example, the consequence of Elena's initial exercise in extortion is that Don Sancho (the young rake whose reputation she exploited in order to extract "compensation" from his uncle and guardian) sets out in pursuit of her, thirsting for revenge. It happens that on the same night as Elena's arrival, he had been on the way to his betrothal when, passing in the street, he caught a fleeting glimpse of a beautiful stranger whose eyes captivate him. Consequently, he abandons his new wife in search of the mysterious stranger and the woman who had tricked his uncle and . . . yes! they are one and the same. When he catches up with Elena, he recognizes the woman of the mysterious glance, and so rage gives way to infatuation. Rather than an innovation, then, we may regard these characteristics of *Elena* as regression to more primitive types of fiction. Most of these observations will apply to Castillo Solórzano also.

Salas moralizes tirelessly. He reproaches his wayward characters like the puppet master directing the sentiments of the audience at his puppets. But although these rhetorical exercises will seem stiff and hollow to our taste, it is worth noting a sample, however briefly, in order to discover what it can tell us about his readers and the very different kind of compact with them which is implied in this novel, in contrast to the earlier picaresque. I take the moment when Sancho is about to desert his wife on his wedding night. Salas interrupts the narrative, and the following sentences occur at about the middle of the author's commentary:

So base is the character of our appetite that it detests the delicate and health-giving foods, but can never have enough of the gross and harmful ones. They set before a prince a dish so exquisite and so elegant that its very aroma gladdens the heart, and if it came with no other sauce than this, it would suffice to restore the spirits of those who have been buried beneath the earth these hundred years. Yet, after looking it over with disdain, and tasting it with more revulsion and finickiness than a newly pregnant girl, he orders them to take it away and to bring up the hash of offal which is got ready for the servants, and sets to it with such a will that he is more like a mule driver who has been traveling since the smiling dawn until nine or ten o'clock at night without eating since breakfast, and who sits down to eat at the inn, so tired and hungry that his hosts will be in trouble if they do not wait upon him speedily and plentifully. . . .

Wretched man, to waste the opportunity to be the most fortunate man on earth! To you Heaven gave the two greatest comforts, the two greatest advantages that human desire can attain, which are an extensive fortune and a wife who is your equal in rank. . . . (902b, 903a)

I make no apology for the translation, since I have deliberately attempted to keep the order and the length of the original Spanish sentences. The passage continues for several more paragraphs yet, dilating upon a situation that, one would have supposed, required no comment at all. It would be easy to assume that, Spain being the puritanical society that it was, an author would feel constrained to condemn aloud all the naughty things his characters did, and that unless he did so the ecclesiastical censor would not write out the customary permit saying the book contained nothing contrary to faith and morals. If we consider such passages carefully, however, we see that they are not only moral judgments but pieces of supplementary characterization. With third-person narration it is not easy, at this period, to get into the character and lay bare the motivation. The only traditional techniques for this had been the set piece monologue and the allegorical projection of the feelings. The first-person narrative, though it restricted the narrator in some obvious ways, gave new opportunities and challenges also. The narrator addressed the reader (or a specific reader) directly, which created a relationship which had to be developed with its revelations, evasions, and strategies of concealment. In particular, Guzmán's analyses of his former self achieve Jamesian complexity. Salas chose not to use that mode of presentation, and found that he had to rely on external commentary. What the commentary does, in addition to condemning Don Sancho's action, is to attempt to make it plausible. As readers, we may find the thought of the newlywedded groom getting out of bed to go and look for the "vile whore" whom he has only glimpsed in the street an unlikely event. Thus the commentary seeks to provide a level of generality ("our human appetites are so perverse that when we have the best we desire the worst") within which the unlikely event can be accommodated. A similar function is performed by proverbs, wise sayings of all kinds, as every reader of *Don Quixote* and of the seventeenth-century drama well knows.

Such a passage as the one we have been considering does something else than place the particular action in a human and moral context, however. A concept such as "depravity" has, we can easily perceive, a *social* connotation. The kind of reader to whom such a novel appealed is indicated by the comparison of foods as well as the quality of person chosen for the analogy. Noble = fine, exquisite; servant = gross, coarse. Levels of taste are grounded on social ones and are appropriate only to that level. For the noble to prefer things that are proper to the churl is depraved; reciprocally, it would be impudent presumption for the low-born picaro to aspire to the things which properly belong to his betters. Finally, there is the display of rhetoric, the facile mastery of long periodic sentences, the sequences of exclamations and rhetorical questions with which the vanity of a new literate readership is flattered. It is not the brilliant, surprising, sometimes overwhelming, but deeply functional rhetoric of Alemán, but conventional embellishment. We find it again in the writing of Castillo Solórzano.

Elena, Daughter of Celestina is not a very good novel, but it typifies the problem of the further development of picaresque literature which, as we have seen, does not proceed by consolidating a stable and replicable genre, but by quantum leaps of virtuosity. If it fails to achieve some new form, it regresses from the qualities that have made it distinctive to other and more easily replicable types of fiction. So it is with *Elena*. A beautiful and seductive adventuress, extortionist, embezzler, whore, and, eventually, murderess, moves among the verbal and structural clichés of polite literature. The author alternately titillates and moralizes. The beautiful criminal fascinates and beguiles, but finishes her career by being garotted and thrown into the river. Her end "stirred pity in the hardest hearts," in contrast to that of her lover who was strung up on the gallows "to the satisfaction of the entire capital" (918b). At the sight of moving events, the deluded characters are prompted to mend their lives, including the young rake, Don Sancho, who decides to love his wife.

III   Castillo Solórzano

The qualities we noted in *Elena, Daughter of Celestina* are present in varying proportions in the works of Don Alonso de Castillo Solórzano, another eclectic writer. (Other works by him have been mentioned in chapter 6.) *The Harpies in Madrid and the Coach of Swindles (Las harpías en Madrid y coche de las estafas*, 1631) gives an indication of how the novel would develop in his hands. To avoid creditors a widow leaves Seville with her two attractive daughters and goes to Madrid where, as a wise old woman tells her, her daughters will be worth a gold mine. In the capital they meet another trio with similar interests. One of the daughters immediately attracts a wealthy young man who negotiates an arrangement with the mother, and from that moment money and expensive gifts are showered upon them. Don Fernando is conveniently killed and the women keep his carriage which becomes the instrument of the swindles which follow. The two sets of women combine their talents and each daughter in turn, with the other women in supporting roles, stages an elaborate confidence trick which, using sex as a bait, separates a man from his money. This is a long way from what we have come to expect of picaresque fiction, and it is not completely typical of Castillo's other female rogue stories. Yet it does portray the pure form of adventure to which they tend, for the sexually baited exploitation of men is the kernel of *Teresa de Manzanares* and *The Wildcat of Seville*, beneath their variety of incident and changes of location. The one constant narrative unit is the confidence trick, involving a degree of calculated theatricality which is not to be found in the *Lazarillo*, except in the activities of the *buldero*, the seller of indulgences.

The *Trickster Girl, Teresa de Manzanares* (*La niña de los embustes, Teresa de Manzanares*, 1632) reverts to the form of the long autobiography, beginning with her mother who is persuaded by a fast talker to leave her village in Galicia and go with him to Madrid. He seduces her on the way and abandons her at an inn. She finds work and eventually a husband in Madrid, and her daughter Teresa grows up lively and mischievous. She learns a craft, making wigs and decorative top knots (materials for deceiving by appearance) and becomes the go-between for the three suitors of her mistress' daughter. She marries an old man for his money and carries on an intrigue with a penniless student. The trick they play on her old husband kills him. Leaving Madrid, she is seized by highway robbers, and nearly raped on the road to Córdoba, then sheltered by a hermit who tells the story of his own disappointment in love which caused him to turn his back on the world. In Córdoba she sets herself up in trade again, then poses as the daughter of the hermit's love who had been captured by Algerian pirates, and is accepted by the father, until the real daughter appears. Moving to Granada she finds that Sarabia (the penniless student) has now become a successful actor, and they are married. Her husband loses money at the gambling table and persuades her to take lovers, "as other actresses do." Sarabia dies from a beating he receives from some quack doctors he mocked, so she marries a rich and very jealous colonial from Peru, and has a risky affair under his nose. He, too, dies and the story continues its succession of deceits, discoveries, false reputations, and fears of public shame. Again she marries, and this time the husband is a miser. We are promised the full story of this in a continuation, which was never published.

Teresa de Manzanares is written clearly, without affectation. But it is obvious that in form it is moving toward a different kind of novel, namely, the long novel of adventures. In that subgenre, Cervantes' *Labors of Persiles and Segismunda* (*Los Trabajos de Persiles y Segismunda*, 1617) is the best known example, and Gonzalo de Céspedes y Meneses, Loubaysín de la Marca, and other writers in the seventeenth century, including Castillo Solórzano himself, had their heroes tangled in complicated adventures by land and sea, captured, shipwrecked, separated from loved ones and reunited after long wanderings, alternately favored and rejected by fortune. Castillo's Teresa meets the person she is impersonating, who belongs in a story told earlier by the hermit; also, she marries the student of the early chapters when he reappears later as a successful actor (chapters 14–15). The autobiographical narration is nonfunctional; it achieves nothing which the third-person narration could not achieve. No reason is given for her addressing the reader, or for Castillo's adopting an inconsistent third-person address in his prologue. Castillo seems to have realized this, because his next long essays in picaresque fiction (*The Adventures of Bachelor Trapaza*; *The Wildcat of Seville*) abandon the first-person viewpoint altogether.

The Wildcat of Seville, Hooker of Purses (*La Garduña de Sevilla y anzuelo de las bolsas*, 1642) is the sequel to *The Adventures of Bachelor Trapaza*, and begins with Estefanía's seeking to procure Trapaza's release from his imprisonment in the galleys. It will be recalled that she had denounced him for his imposture as a Portuguese aristocrat. After his release, they are married, but he returns to his gambling and Estefanía dies of disappointment. Their daughter, Rufina, grows up mischievous and willful, as we might expect. She marries an old colonial and deceives him first with a man who cheats her with the gift of a beautiful dress that he has borrowed. When her father hears of this he duels with the man and is killed. Another lover presents himself, and kills the first in a duel beneath the husband's window. The latter hears everything they say, and dies of chagrin. Left without money, Rufina now enters into a partnership with Garay, an old associate of her father Trapaza, and this partnership gives her the opportunity to work more ingenious swindles than she could do on her own. They arrive at the house of Marquina, a rich colonial, and she spins a story about a tragic love which ended with her lover being killed and herself pursued by her father and the officers of justice. The rich man's house, hidden in the country outside Seville, is just the place for her to hide. He swallows the story and offers her his house. Her beauty and her tears also cause him to fall in love with her, as she expected that he would, and so he is an easy victim. She and Garay, who poses as her squire, stay long enough to get to know the house and its contents,

and to gain the old man's confidence. They next rob a Genoese
merchant, gaining his confidence by pretending to share his interest
in alchemy, after which they take to the road. On the way, they hear
some robbers talking about their leader, Crispín, who has escaped
detection by masquerading as a pious hermit. Rufina sees another
opportunity here, so she plays the part of a damsel in distress. Garay
ties her to a tree within earshot of Crispín's hut, where she de-
claims, "Will no one help an unlucky woman who is about to lose
her life? Have pity on me, oh heavens! and avenge my wronged
innocence!" Garay plays the part of the heartless attacker: "Com-
mend yourself to God in the short time you have to live, for as soon
as I've finished tying you to this tree, I'm going to stab you to death"
(1574b). As they had planned, Crispín rushes forth to rescue her.
Predictably, he also falls in love with her and entertains her lavishly,
while she learns the amount of his loot and of his plans for future
assaults. Eventually, she and Garay are able to betray the whole
gang into the hands of the law, concealing the loot for themselves.
The robbers are hanged, but Crispín escapes, so Rufina and Garay
have to thwart his desires for revenge. He reappears in disguise,
and attempts to use a handsome young man, Jaime, as decoy. But
Jaime, like every other man, falls in love with Rufina, and she with
him, so they trap Crispín who is captured and executed. Garay, who
is no longer necessary to Rufina, or to the author, is caught thieving
and sent to the galleys. Rufina and Jaime move to Saragossa where
she opens a shop, selling silks.

Like Salas Barbadillo's *Elena*, Castillo's *Wildcat* moves in the
direction of the *novela cortesana*. The first-person narration, which
was simply routine picaresque convention in *Teresa de Manzanares*,
and wholly lacking in function, has now been abandoned. The
presence of Rufina's father Trapaza, a survivor from an earlier novel,
has little relation with the burden of heredity and of family example
which characterized earlier novels. He is given a violent death
(poetic justice, no doubt), but without fuss. Castillo was himself an
accomplished practitioner of the *novela cortesana;* he knew the
formulas, and which ones could be applied to his hybrid picaresque
narratives. His romantic novels are diversified in various ways, by
the secondary characters who tell of their own breath-taking escapes
and passionate amorous intrigues, or by the introduction of incidental entertainments. These most frequently take the form of an
after-dinner story told by one of the company, or verses sung on

some occasion (and miraculously recalled by the narrator). The singer is usually the heroine herself, whose voice is invariably exquisite. In *Teresa de Manzanares* are included the texts of two short farces. *The Wildcat of Seville* has a story told by one of Crispín's robber band, as well as the lyrics sung by Rufina in the house of Octavio, the Genoese merchant, the better to captivate him.

We should also note that Castillo moves the plot in the direction of the novel of love and adventure. This is done by sleight of hand, when Rufina impersonates the kind of person who has a leading role in such novels. In order to trick Marquina she poses as the perse- cuted victim of a drama of love and honor, and she engineers her "rescue" by Crispín, playing the maiden in distress. This situation is also explained by an invented story of love and revenge. Even when she is not acting, Rufina is made to look less like a female rogue, and more like the heroine of romance. This is not to say that she is less intrinsically criminal or dangerous or immoral than Trapaza or Teresa, but that she is set up against others who are worse than she is. As soon as she begins scheming to betray the robber gang which has sheltered her, the right-thinking reader knows whom to cheer. Any scruples we may have about the abuse of hospitality melt away before an offense which is far worse, the cloaking of crime with religion. And when Crispín escapes and seeks revenge, she effec- tively becomes the heroine, not by virtue but by opposition. The reader is with her because she has an enemy. She obviously does not possess the qualities of the conventional heroine (except beauty and wit, and she needs these for her own unladylike devices), but she is put into the role of heroine by a shifting of the balance within the novel. But having watched her feign the role of heroine and seen the mantle descend adventitiously upon her, we are the less sur- prised, perhaps, when she reaps the kind of reward usually reserved for true fictional heroines: she marries and settles down with the man she loves. This is still not quite a *novela cortesana* ending, since they have to run away to Saragossa in order to escape the victims of their latest mischief. Finally, Castillo assures us that the two worlds (of romance by birthright, and romance by fraud) are not really interchangeable, when the couple set themselves up in the retail trade. That is something that the best people would not do.

The world of values in Castillo's fiction is a peculiar one. Almost every act, however monstrous, is conceived as a joke *(burla)* and almost any person may become the object of one. Rufina's robberies are jokes. Teresa's acts of revenge are jokes. In *Teresa de Manzanares* there is a young man who is in love with a girl, but she does not repay his love. Instead, she has a hopeless attachment to a choirboy who is a castrato (Spanish, *capón*). In the literature of this period castrati, hunchbacks, nearsighted persons, dwarfs—in short, all those who fall short of a Hollywood standard of physique—are fair game, so Teresa sees fit to play a joke on this youth by claiming to have invented a lotion that will give him a manly beard. This promised remedy is a bottle of acid, which will leave him disfigured for the rest of his life. This *burla*, and another ingenious little piece of cruelty directed against quack doctors, are presented to us a second time, transformed into short dramatic farces. (They are included in chapters 12 and 16.) Each one of Rufina's depredations in *The Wildcat* is also seen, contrary to the moralizing, as another joke and made palatable or even justified for her readers, perhaps, by some moral or physical imperfection in her victim. An example of the moral compensation, so to speak, of the immoral act can be seen in the treatment of Marquina after Rufina has ransacked his house. Usually, as soon as the theft (or other "joke") has been committed, Rufina decamps and the narrator follows her, and no more attention is paid to the victim. But on this occasion we are told, with some complacency, that the loss of his property and his hopes of gaining Rufina drove him crazy and that, because he was very stingy, almost everyone in Seville was pleased. Here and elsewhere Castillo would have us believe that Rufina is performing a public service.

In the prologue to each of these volumes, Castillo claims that he is holding up his protagonist as a warning, a negative example to be shunned:

Teresa de Manzanares reveals herself and her tricks to the eyes of all. Her mischief is to be a warning to you to shun all who follow her profession. . . . (1343b)

The reader may take warning from her of evils which can be avoided, by being forewarned against deceit, abstaining from vice, and shunning this licentious way of life and these low-born natures. (1344a)

Let this living portrait of what happens with women of this sort [i.e., Rufina] serve as a warning to the reader. I have made a composite picture so that the reckless may be warned, the careless take heed; I do not set down fantastic inventions, but the condition of our times. . . . (1529a)

Anyone who took such protestations seriously would soon be perplexed by the frequency with which Teresa's tiresome husbands drop dead, and everyone except Rufina gets caught. On the other hand, the activities of his invulnerable protagonists are not of a different order from those of the antagonists. The similarity between the way Rufina sets up rich Marquina to fall in love with her so that she can rob him, and the way that Crispin sets up Rufina to fall in love with his decoy, Jaime (*Wildcat*, books 1, 4) provides an instructive comparison. Rufina's ploy works, but Crispín's does not. Rufina gets the gold, Crispín gets the gallows. These are but the most obvious contradictions which derive from attempting to impose moral discriminations upon an amoral, success-oriented plot.

Castillo also sprinkles moralities over his narrative, but he is less prodigal with them than Salas Barbadillo was. He is also less consistent, but this is a failure of art rather than of ethics. For example, when Rufina marries a rich, retired colonial, we know that she is bound to deceive him. We may suspect it on the basis of what we know of her nature, but we also know from literary experience that the marriage of a young woman and an aging man is one of the basic situations of comedy and farce, and as such it is a given story type, beyond good and evil. So basic is it that the reader is willing to accept it as a matter of dynamics, an unstable situation to be judged by what seem to him to be the universal standards of nature rather than of morals. Such a story may, of course, be transformed by human sympathy and moral depth, and this is what Cervantes aimed to achieve in his story of *El celoso extremeño (The Jealous Extremaduran)*. Castillo was interested only in the episodic development and the comic exploitation of this story, so it is incongruous to weigh the situation in a solemn little aside about fathers who marry their daughters with an unequal match (1533–34). Her father, Trapaza, is killed in a duel by one of her lovers: "the two of them drew their swords, but it went against Trapaza, and that was his last day. With a thrust of his sword, Roberto left him expiring and unable to make any act of contrition. Those who live as he did come to this kind of end" (1533b). In this event we see an example of how Castillo overdetermines the response of the reader. If he wished to make the point that bad livers come to a bad end, was it necessary to press so hard? And does not Rufina herself contradict the point? We know that it is not true in real life, but we accept it in fiction so long as it is sold to us as an ideal truth, not a practical one. I said that the failure is one of art and not of morals, because amusing tales of unscrupulous adventurers are a popular tradition of story-telling, and the sharp-witted, opportunistic hero is characteristic of every culture's oral literature. A large part of the appeal of such stories lies in our desire to be free from restraints, and our admiration for the man or woman who can act with unconcern for conventional warnings illustrates part of the thesis developed by Freud in his *Civilization and Its Discontents*. The addition to such stories of censorious warnings and I told you so's, is more than a breach of literary decorum and consistency: it suggests an audience who, like the author, is uncertain of its values, but formalistic and conventional in morality, desiring that the free-floating traditional fictional motifs be pinned down with moral labels.

IV   The Picaresque Woman: Conclusions

There was little room for women in the life of the male picaro. In *Lazarillo de Tormes* we see the two universally fundamental female roles of mother and wife at the beginning and the end, but we scarcely glimpse the women who play these roles. After the disappearance of the father, Lazarillo's mother moved from the mill to a noble household where she worked as a menial servant and formed a sexual liaison with a negro stablehand. Lázaro's "success story" is perhaps surpassed in irony by the composite female figures of the beginning and end: *his* wife succeeds in being both wife and mistress simultaneously! In between these two there are some kindly neighbors who give food to Lazarillo (chapter 3), and some provocatively veiled women by the river, whom the squire engages in amorous conversation, and who leave him as soon as they discover he is penniless. Guzmán and Pablos also encounter courtesans; Guzmán marries, and prostitutes his wife. Not surprisingly, the male picaro encounters women in the few roles which the society of the time allowed: wife, mother, and a few trades, such as keeping an inn or a lodging house, and seamstress. Beyond these few roles lay the chaotic, lawless outer world of prostitutes, procuresses, and camp followers. In the stratified and hierarchical world of the early seventeenth century, social mobility could still carry threatening connotations of disorder, of the breakdown of a given system of authority and obedience, so that the reader of picaresque novels can hardly avoid being aware of this. If such was the case with the picaresque male, the position of women, tied functionally to male social roles, was even less flexible. Female roles were static: wife, mother, provider. Even inns,which dissolved social boundaries and put people in tempting proximity to one another, could be a gate into that unruly outer world where freedom was a synonym for licentiousness.

Considered in purely literary terms, the emergence of the *picara*, or female rogue, seems to promise the most interesting stroke of originality in a series of novels which are outstanding for their continual innovations. But the realities of social life, which we have just mentioned, impose severe limitations on such possibilities. In this sense the picaresque novel may fairly be called realistic, the availability of female roles corresponding closely, at the appropriate social level, to that of the real world. Justina's parents are innkeepers, and much of her story is about others, rather than about herself. Castillo's Teresa also begins as a servant in an inn, and inns have always served in fiction as a window on the wider world, a congeries of persons who would not normally be accessible to the narrator in one place. But the inn remains stationary, and the inn servant can have only the illusion of movement, like a boat moored in the stream. It is apposite, then, that the female rogue starts her career there, because of the inn's double significance, representing the female tradition of service in a confined social space, and a point of departure into a wider and more questionable world.

Since the social parameters of a woman's career in that world were so narrow, it was almost inevitable that the picara should be as restricted in the kinds of activities available to her as the domestic woman was. "The genre . . . required a protagonist who would move more or less freely through the strata of society," wrote Thomas Hanrahan, "but the female protagonist, the picara, is really an impossibility and the nearest approach is the swindler."[8] Consequently, this variation on the picaresque theme runs its course and exhausts itself rapidly. The male protagonist plays out a drama of tensions between freedom and entrapment, responsibility and determinism, high aspirations and sordid accommodations. It is difficult to see how a picara could have faced similar tensions without exposing the unexposable, the traditionally venerated roles of womanhood, wife and mother. Perhaps the minor, if crucial, roles of mother and wife in the world of the male picaro were as far as the novelists felt they could go. At any rate, neither Salas Barbadillo nor Castillo Solórzano had the talent to uncover significance in com-

monplace situations and small compromises, as the anonymous author of *Lazarillo* and as Alemán did. So through the picaresque
woman the novel turns into literature of crude entertainment, dis-
playing jokers and swindlers of a criminal or near-criminal sort, who
commit only such acts of violence as accord with the prejudices of
the readers. Whereas *Lazarillo de Tormes* and *Guzmán de Alfarache*
sharpen consciousness, these novels dull it. The ingenuity is
superficial, the moral vision confused. When one sees added to the
enormously profitable swindles the sexual bait and the expensive
prostitution in *The Harpies in Madrid,* one wonders what the Inquisition's censors really meant when they wrote the customary
approval, and commended the author for warning Spanish youth
against the false song of those sirens.[9]

One of the marks of originality of the Spanish picaresque novel
was to have broken down the barriers which literary theorists in the
sixteenth century had erected between styles (low or high) and
subject matter (comic or serious). Novelists like Salas Barbadillo and
Castillo Solórzano were regressive in this respect. Their styles were
linked consistently with an evaluation of stylistic level in terms of
social class: low-born characters are funny, incapable of true love,
unworthy of sympathy, whereas the nobler and richer ones (so long
as their money is not derived from retail trade) are capable of
fineness of feeling and of the most dramatic moral improvement on
the impulse of a good example or a fearful warning. Characters and
situations are repeated and become clichés, such as the fraudulent
hermits who populate the picaresque landscape. Or stock situations
of sentimental fiction are taken up and transposed, like finding a
tearful lady tied to a tree. "Illusionist," "unhistorical," and "unsub-
stantial" are epithets applied by a recent writer to the picaresque
works of Castillo Solórzano, and it would be difficult to protest that
he is too severe.[10]

CHAPTER 8

Review and Conclusions

W E now turn to the questions which have accompanied us in
the course of this book: what are the distinctive qualities of
Spanish picaresque literature, and can they be systematized to the
point where we can satisfactorily speak of a picaresque genre with a
history and a coherent and stable identity? How important are
historical and social factors to a proper understanding of individual
novels and to the persistence of the type?

Fonger de Haan, the first modern scholar to write at length on the
picaresque, has a succinct definition: "the autobiography of a *picaro*,
a rogue, and in that form a satire upon the conditions and persons of
the time that gives it birth."[1] This is restated a few pages later with
some additional elements: "It is the prose autobiography of a person, real or imaginary, who strives by fair means and by foul to make
a living, and in relating his experiences in various classes of society,
points out the evils which come under his observation" (8). The
essential features would seem to be: autobiography ("real or imaginary"), the antiheroic character of the protagonist and his actions,
the various classes of society, and the satirical or critical observation.
The qualification as to autobiography allows Estebanillo González to
be included, but our reading of that work has shown that it is not all
one whether the life be real or imaginary. The social observation
presupposes social mobility, and the criticism and satire of "evils"
imply a moral position. F. W. Chandler shares the same perceptions but with a more noticeable tendency to schematize, although
he writes at greater length. Thus, the picaro is the "best instrument
for satire" because "his point of view was precisely the opposite of
the ordinary observer's. What he praised was infallibly blameworthy, what he blamed was really meritorious."[2] As a result, "the
values of the good and the bad . . . by this new device stood forth
again sharply defined" (43). He also adds to this typology of the

134

picaro a concept of historical development: the "emergence of personality." Beginning with *Pablos the Cheat (El Buscón)*, says Chandler, is a second stage "in which less attention was paid to the classes of society and more to the observer." We look on his rogueries "not as mere tricks, but as expressing himself and contributing to a plot" (272). Chandler's book was influential for the next half century and remains the most extensive work in English on the subject, yet it contains a quantity of misleading rhetoric. "What he praised was infallibly blameworthy, what he blamed was really meritorious" is an effective epigram but it just is not true, because most picaros are not given to praising and blaming. The exceptions, Guzmán de Alfarache, Alonso (he of the many masters), do not *write* as picaros but as censors: their praise and blame are not reversible. Indeed, Guzmán's book is a vast catalog of self-blame. *Romances of Roguery* also has an evolutionary bias in its concept of "emergence of personality" and the implication that "expressing himself" is a higher stage of artistic development. It is summed up in the phrase "the inevitable progression of fiction from events toward character" (272). We are not now committed to the idea that any such progression in literature is inevitable; in particular, such a progression seems strangely inapplicable as a way of evaluating the tricky enterprises of a Trapaza or a Teresa de Manzanares, which do not express character at all, but their author's impulse to imagine swindles. When progressions are accepted as inevitable, genre is perceived as changing, not as cumulative, and there is then no reason to ask whether changes are compatible with some basic or essential model of the genre.

The decline of the idea of evolutionary progress in literature brought a new search for meaning in the picaresque, and that meaning was to be located in a prototype, one example of peculiar distinction and expressive value, which could be said to establish patterns of structure and an authoritative subject matter. The desire for a model tended to bring into relief the qualities in later fiction which did not conform to it, and these differences were not always minor ones. The principal difficulty lay in reconciling *Lazarillo de Tormes* and *Guzmán de Alfarache*. If one takes *Lazarillo* as the prototype, *Guzmán* with all its sermons and divagations and its sheer size is not just a wandering boy story vastly inflated, but a monstrous deviation. On the other hand, if *Guzmán* is perceived as the model by reason both of its extended action and the complexity

from *Lazarillo*. From then on, a set of options exist for subsequent writers, and these options constitute the paradigm.[5]

The solution to the problem of genre which is propounded by Lázaro, Guillén, and Francisco Rico, among others, is to place *Guzmán de Alfarache* over *Lazarillo de Tormes* and to say that where the formal elements coincide, there is the essential structure of the genus picaresque. Yet, as we have seen, the tensions between *Lazarillo* and *Guzmán* are as evident as are the correspondences; indeed, the very correspondences are the means by which oppositions are both concealed and expressed. Apart from the very obvious differences of size and scale, we might consider the scarcely less obvious differences of narrative plot. Is it fair to present the brief story of a young boy who is raised in poverty and given away as a servant as being formally identical with the very long story of a boy who is raised in luxury and leaves home by his own choice? Clearly, picaresque is not as easy to define as it appeared to be at the beginning of this century: the career of a knave, and a gallery of satirical portraits. Alemán pressed the narrative of Guzmán's life beyond all conceivable boundaries of mere knavery as it is commonly understood when he made him commit the least public, the most intimate forms of dishonesty; with oneself, with one's wife, with one's God.

The "modal" approach suggested by Robert Scholes[6] and extended by Ulrich Wicks,[7] in which picaresque is located between satire and comedy, on a spectrum which extends from satire to romance with history at the midpoint, is more ambitious. It aims to present a map of all possible types of fiction in such a way that we can explain "shades and mixtures," how "in any particular work of narrative fiction . . . several of the ideal types of literature are mixed together to achieve the uniqueness of that work."[8] This has the virtue of flexibility, relieves us of the difficulties of drawing boundaries, while allowing that certain motifs (freedom/entrapment; primitive survival; role changing, for example) may recur with great frequency. This system also follows tradition in referring the fictional world to a concept of better, worse than, or about equal to the world as we know it, with picaresque occurring in a world recognizably worse, more chaotic than ours. Literary theories, however, are like fictions: indeed, in a manner of speaking they are fictions. They do not relieve us of the difficulty of deciding to what degree and with what fidelity the fictional and the real correspond.

It is *assumed* that the picaresque "world" occupies a certain evalua-
tive level in relation to ours, but the first-person viewpoint inevitably calls this into question. Again, the theory will not tell us how
largely a given motif has to figure, or whether it has to figure at all,
before we call a fiction genuinely picaresque, or only a picaresque
"shading" of something else.

Picaresque novels are often described as "realistic" because they
show dirt and beggars and describe places and persons in whose real
existence we could believe. We also, being human, find it easier to
believe in the baser motives of others than in noble ones. But no
novel ever presents a complete picture of the external world, and
our use of the word "picture" at once betrays our expectation of an
order, a sense of selection and arrangement that the real world does
not have until we filter it through our trained expectations.
Lazarillo's social classes are represented only by the meanest individuals. Literature is "real" in relation to norms, not to life.[9] The
long debate about the relation of picaresque literature to social
conditions is bound to remain inconclusive for this reason. Any
modern urban society—and picaresque literature represents a predominantly urban society—offers opportunities for success to the
unscrupulous, whether the times are lean or fat. Which social facts
should these novels be referred to in order to extract their social
significance? Marcel Bataillon referred *Lazarillo* to the debates on
vagrancy and how to control it, from 1530 on.[10] The years from 1530
to 1580 were a period of increasing population: they were also a
period of expansion in industry and agriculture.[11]

Economic depression in the period 1595–1621 might appear to
offer an explanation for the wandering picaro in search of a meal.
But then a succession of plagues between 1596 and 1600, produced
an acute shortage of labor[12] so that an equilibrium was maintained.
There is no simple correspondence between picaresque literature
and lack of work or general proverty: "the picaresque flourished in
the period of Castile's maximum prosperity, when there was a
demand for labor and wages were high. It is wrong, therefore to see
in it the reflection of a economic and social order; rather it is the
description of urban outcasts who exist in any affluent society."[13] It
would be equally mistaken, for the same reason, to see *Lazarillo* as a
protest against the slowness of the rise in standards in a period of
economic boom.[14] Hunger is universally experienced and poverty is
always locally present somewhere: hunger and poverty are always

available therefore as universal imaginative symbols of the human condition. Indeed, hunger may be the more necessary and effective as a literary theme in times of arrogant wealth and material satisfaction. As Schiller observed in *Die Weltweisen*, "hunger and love are what moves the world."

Two books which have recently appeared, both of them interesting in their different ways, illustrate the limitations of what we might call the traditional historicist approach, which has been with us at least since the late eighteenth century in its capsular formulation that "literature is an expression of society." Alan Francis, in *Picaresca, decadencia, historia* (1978) sets out to examine the progress of the picaresque novel in terms of the commonly expressed notion of Spain's decadence in the seventeenth century. Did the novel reflect the decline in society and politics? Did the novel itself share in that decline? Analyzing the presentation of "the three dominant themes" of honor, religion, and the vision of Spain, in two groups of novels ("picaresca inicial" and "picaresca decadente," the second being subdivided into "conformistas" and "problemáticos"), some interesting observations emerge. But, of course, the importance of the result will depend on the correctness of the prior selection of the "dominant themes," on the clear understanding and critical exposition of the concept of "decline," and on an awareness that a theme in fiction does not necessarily transpose that same theme from real life in the same form and intensity and prominence, since literature is not reportage. Too much is here taken for granted.

Richard Bjornson's book is more ambitious, both because he proposes to study the European versions of picaresque, and because his conceptual scheme seems to promise more. His book is grounded on two givens: first, that the picaresque novel is to be interpreted as a response to changes in the class structure of society, and second, that there is an "essential picaresque situation" which takes the form of "the paradigmatic confrontation between an isolated individual and a hostile society" (4). Among the novels themselves, he finds two groups: those in which character is "given," a fact of nature "to be tested and revealed for what it is during the course of the fictional hero's adventures" (e.g., *Pablos The Cheat, Pícara Justina; Marcos de Obregón*), and those others in which "character is susceptible to a socializing process" (e.g., *Lazarillo de Tormes; Guzmán de Alfarache;* Defoe's *Moll Flanders*) (11–12). Once more, the method is called into question by its neatness.

The fictional world evoked within the novel is identified too easily with the society outside it. Imagined societies may serve very different purposes than reflecting the real world, even when they resemble it in many particulars, and may serve very different purposes from novel to novel, even when they closely resemble one another. The changes in class structure which form the "background" of the picaresque novel are the by now familiar rise of the middle class, the emergence of bourgeois individualism, and the consequent redefinition of values (4). This, however, is a process which had been going on in Europe since the fourteenth century; is it, then, the background to which picaresque should be related if we are to understand its special relevance to its moment in time? Anyone who reads the voluminous historiography of the last twenty years, especially the writings on what has come to be known as the "crisis of the seventeenth century," and the formidable attempts to construct a sociology of the period, will find such a formula as the "rise of the middle class" unsatisfactory, to say the least.[15] When we turn our attention from the real society to the imagined world of the novels, the phrase "hostile society" is too simplistic a formula to represent the enormously variable relations between the protagonist and other people, not only from novel to novel, but within the same novel. Consciously or unconsciously, Bjornson seems to be trying to make a scientific approach, reducing the data to two constants and one variable. The best things in this book—and I am not saying it has no merit—come when he shakes himself free from the shackles of some determinist assumptions.[16]

It is legitimate to put the question of the relation to society in a different form, and ask what in Spanish culture of the early seventeenth century disposed the public to receive antichivalrous novels, in which the protagonist refuses the established roles and the traditional paths to self-esteem. The converso problem was one source of social tensions.[17] There were other kinds of stress in social relations, which multiplied and deepened as small landowners were ruined by large magnates, towns lost their independence to those same magnates, and the crown supported aristocratic interests against the small peasants and tradesmen. There was the increasingly centralized, anonymous character of urban culture and administration, together with the rapid growth of cities and their transformation from recognizable communities with representative government into tense battlegrounds between the old nobility and the new rich as they struggled for power and competed in ostentation. Traditional forms and structures in social relations which had been invested with security and value were dissolving, and new rigid barriers were forming, new coercive patterns which would be felt as arbitrary and inhuman.[18] In earlier fiction, the principal characters were stable, their status being inseparable from their identity: a knight, a priest, a merchant, a prince, a poet, a man of law, etc. This is not so in picaresque. The picaro is someone on the move, a boy who is *becoming* what he is not yet, a man seeking to be other than what he is. From the point of view of social existence, the picaro is he who is not.

Whatever the tide of critical fashion may bring, the peculiar literary-historical circumstance of picaresque—the sudden passage from never-never lands of chivalrous romance or timeless bucolic landscapes echoing with complaints of love, to urban subworlds of cheating and gambling and knowing one trick more than the devil—has made it inevitably an object of historical and sociological study. As we indicated earlier, in this chapter and in those on *Lazarillo* and *Guzmán,* the positivist attempt to relate picaresque fiction to precise economic and social facts, as the product of those facts, has proved to be illusory.[19] In recent years, however, some more fruitful sociological criticism has appeared, following the brilliant examples of György Lukács and Lucien Goldmann.[20] The revolutionary impact which structural anthropology has had on sociology enabled Goldmann to extend Lukács' perception of the relation between art and social consciousness in the following terms:

. . . since Lukács sought out the interconnection between creation and social consciousness not in the contents but in *the categories which structure one or other of them,* and above all in their consistency, the research inspired by him is free from these objections [i.e., of fragmenting the work, highlighting whatever is a direct reproduction of reality and disregarding everything which has to do with imaginative creation]. The same categories and the same consistency may govern worlds with *completely different contents,* so that the transposition by the imagination is no longer an obstacle to the existence of a close relation between culture and society.[21]

Sociocriticism (a term translated from the French *sociocritique*) has appeared, and the Spanish picaresque novels have received attention from its practitioners (Brun, Ferreras, Cros). Cros in particular, in a series of essays on Quevedo's *Buscón,* has attempted to make a semiotic analysis of the text yield the underlying ideology which shapes the linguistic and structural elements in the novel.[22] It is not clear that the results are any more scientific than earlier criticism, in the sense of dispensing with analytical tools which themselves imply value, and free from circularity. But it does at least eschew the impressionistic use of historical background as a way of conflating the truth of a novel. And it may enable us to see more clearly the originality of writers who evoked in their novels a world which was sensitive to the parameters of real society as far as the individual's range of action was concerned, but was also a verbal artifact made by the protagonist to nurture and protect his self-image. The picaro may be a creature of society, but he also incorporates society in his experience of it. And since the picaro is the writer, it may be his view of it, rather than society itself which is problematic, because the nature and significance of his society are established retroactively as that which enhances his own nature and significance, to himself. The social world in these novels is, in part at least, a symbolic projection of the picaro's own desires.[23]

In the autobiographical fictions, we are less interested in the external aspects of the action in the long run, however "real" they may appear, than in the question: how does this protagonist become this story-teller? What is the link, the means by which the impulsive *liver* becomes the self-conscious *teller* of his life? In each case we recognize the presence of an authority ("Your Honor"; "the Reader," "the Public") and the picaro transforms himself into narrator in obedience to that authority as he perceives it, or as he has internalized it. There is thus in each of these novels a hidden authority, and an act of obedience to that authority in the form of a self-justification. The disordered chaos of his life is given form in response to a higher will. From this perspective, such narratives may be seen to be conservative in ideology rather than disruptive.

In the section on *Marcos de Obregón*, I suggested that each writer encountered in the preceding novels a bundle of possibilities which could be freely exploited, rather than a genre whose integrity had to be preserved. So, in *Estebanillo González*, the fictional autobiography has served as an enabling model, by virtue of which it is possible to write self-disparagingly about what seems to have been a real life. Fiction has been made the precedent for a new kind of autobiography. Other writers take the picaresque impulse in other directions. There are books on prison life and the risks of city life.[24]

A long narrative poem, The *Life of the Picaro (La vida del pícaro)* celebrates the picaresque life for its lack of cares, freedom from odious responsibilities, and opportunities for ingenuity.[25] Alcalá Yáñez' *Alonso* preserves the autobiographical form and the conversion from *Guzmán*, whereas Espinel's *Marcos de Obregón* has blended real life and fiction but without the ignoble protagonist. Yet other novelists—Salas Barbadillo, Castillo Solórzano—develop the ignoble protagonist as a generator of ingenious swindles and almost nothing more. The successes of these characters enable them to stay for a time in a wealthy aristocratic milieu which flatters the readers. Meantime, picaresque episodes become a standard form of variation in the novels of love and adventure like Céspedes y Meneses' *Varia fortuna del soldado Píndaro*. There is no simple progression: the movement is centrifugal rather than linear, pulling away from the original core of autobiography, ignoble hero, cyclical pattern of events. If there is one quality which characterizes the picaresque in Spain it is a relationship which is not conformity to a model, but disconformity. Those works which we can see were most original are most antagonistic to their predecessors in the way that they make shared formal elements signify something radically different.

Even without giving special attention to later non-Spanish literature, we can see how the Spanish exemplars contain many of the disturbing features familiar to us in modern fiction. Picaresque was, as I think the evidence compels us to conclude, the genre which denied itself, contradicted and finally destroyed itself, and as such it sets in motion a process which may be obscured in the eighteenth century but which in the nineteenth and twentieth centuries becomes the typical expression of artistic energy: "a novel characteristically opposes other novels. This is not say that novelists are not formally indebted to other novelists, but that the rules of the game forbid overt acknowledgement of this debt, except in the form of parody."[26] Allegorical romance had struggled for its living space against heroic epic, and chivalric romance against the allegorical, and so on. The Spanish writers of picaresque were the first to discover that the novel (though the name did not yet exist), which justifies itself by an ongoing renunciation of the dogmatics of "art" and ever-renewed claims on "reality," exists in a peculiar relation to itself. The more artifice it sheds, the more it generates within itself, and it incorporates reality only by making it literary in spite of itself.

The adoption of an autobiographical mode of presentation was the most potent gesture of renunciation of the dogmatics of art, since it challenges the reality of generic boundaries. Max Frisch, whose works make the boundaries between fiction and autobiography unreal, makes us think of *Marcos de Obregón, Estebanillo González,* and, by implication, all the other works which we believe are on the fiction side of the invisible boundary when he writes: "The selection of facts, representing an intent, already means interpretation, and it is not important whether the material is fictional or factual."[27] Other kinds of dogmatics are threatened by the autobiographical mode, since it raises the possibility that candor may come to replace more traditional ethical values as the support for subject matter, and may even become a theme in its own right. Autobiography makes a new relativism accessible to fiction. Augustine's "Give me chastity and continence, but not yet" (*Confessions,* book 8, chapter 7) had been acceptable within a pattern of Christian heroism: conversion as a turning around; the sequence obstinacy/submission/exaltation; the enemy who becomes the champion of the faith. It is only in the light of this later exaltation and vindication that what Christians would have called a "blasphemy against the spirit" can be tolerated. But suppose there were no vindication, and no desire to be cleansed or exalted? The conservatism of Alemán, which we noticed earlier, becomes apparent once more as he attempts to crush the disturbing possibilities created by *Lazarillo* under the enormous weight of rhetorically elaborated spiritual introspections and moral commentaries, and reshape them to the epic pattern of conversion and rebirth into a new level of consciousness which subsumes the old life. The originality of *Lazarillo* is apparent in many ways, but in one way it is supreme and absolute: its story is not simply the disreputable doings of the narrator, but the formulation of a corrupt consciousness, which is that of the narrator. It is obvious that in a literary tradition which located narrative point of view within the firmly grounded moral consciousness of the narrator (whether first or third person makes no difference here), *Lazarillo* was intensely subversive. Perhaps it was too subversive as art to be recognized as such until Alemán and Cervantes and Quevedo played their brilliant responses around it.

Notes and References

Chapter One

1. Alberto del Monte, *Itinerario de la novela picaresca* (Barcelona: Ed. Lumen, 1971), p. 11; Yakov Malkiel, "El núcleo del problema etimológico de *picaro-picardía*," in *Studia Hispanica in Honorem R. Lapesa*, vol. 2 (Madrid: Gredos, 1974), pp. 307–42.
2. Malkiel, pp. 340–42.
3. See ibid.

Chapter Two

1. Claudio Guillén, ed., *Lazarillo de Tormes* and *El Abencerraje* (New York: Dell, 1966), p. 33. This whole question is discussed in Francisco Rico, "En torno al texto crítico del *L de T*," *Hispanic Review*, 38 (1970), 405–19; Alberto Blecua in his ed. of *L de T* (Madrid: Castalia, 1974). Also, see the introduction to Rico's *La novela picaresca*.
2. Marcel Bataillon, *Novedad y fecundidad del L de T* (Salamanca: Anaya, 1968), pp. 27–45; Fernando Lázaro Carreter, *L de T en la picaresca* (Barcelona: Ariel, 1972), pp. 64–122, are principal sources for this section.
3. In *Hacia Cervantes*, 3d ed. (Madrid: Taurus, 1967), p. 146.
4. R. O. Jones, introduction to his edition of *L de T* (Manchester: Manchester University Press, 1963), p. xxxviii.
5. *L de T: A Critical Guide* (London: Grant & Cutler, 1975), p. 32.
6. Bataillon, *Novedad*, p. 67.
7. Deyermond, *Critical Guide*, chap. 4.
8. F. Lázaro Carreter, pp. 98–102.
9. Ibid., passim.
10. E.g., Guillén introduction to his edition; Francisco Rico's *La novela picaresca y el punto de vista* (Barcelona: Seix Barral, 1970), pp. 21–25.
11. A suggestion also made by Richard Hitchcock, "Lazarillo and Vuestra Merced," *MLN*, 86 (1971), 264–66.
12. Deyermond, p. 94.
13. Luna may have intended his continuation to be used as a reading text by his students of Spanish. See Richard Bjornson, *The Picaresque Hero in*

147

European   Fiction (Madison: University of Wisconsin Press, 1977),
pp. 97–98.
   14. Bataillon studies the continuations concisely in *Novedad*, chap. 6.
   15. For example, Martin de Riquer, ed., *La Celestina y Lazarillos* (Barcelona: Vergara, 1959), p. 133.
   16. Del Monte, *Itinerario*, p. 114.
   17. Bjornson, *Picaresque Hero*, pp. 99–100.

Chapter Three

   1. For the life of Alemán see Donald McGrady, *Mateo Alemán* (New
York: Twayne, 1968); Edmond Cros, *Mateo Alemán: Introducción a su vida
y a su obra* (Salamanca: Anaya, 1971), and "La vie de Mateo Alemán:
Quelques documents inédits. Quelques suggestions," *Bulletin Hispanique*,
72 (1970), 331–37. All the statements that Alemán was a converso lead back
ultimately to F. Rodríguez Marín, "Documentos referentes a Mateo Alemán y a sus deudos más cercanos," *Boletín de la Real Academia Española*,
20 (1933), 167–217 (also published separately [Madrid: Tipografía Archivos,
1933], Rodríguez Marín promised (note to final document) to publish the
evidence for his assertion, but never did so. Of the author's mother, whose
name was changed in one document, Marín states that "in Seville, with a
name like that—Enero—you could tell she was Jewish a hundred leagues
off ["olía a judío a cien leguas"]. In fact, her name was Italian: see Claudio
Guillén, "Los pleitos extremeños de Mateo Alemán, I. El Juez, 'Dios de la
tierra,' " *Archivo Hispalense*, 32 (1960), 387–407, and her Florentine connections are known. This should have reduced Marín's credibility, but
apparently has not. In the fifteenth century there were both Jews and
non-Jews bearing the name Alemán (meaning "German") in Seville, which
attracted German artisans, including the first printers in Spain; see Eugenio
Asensio, "La peculiaridad literaria de los conversos," *Anuario de estudios
medievales*, 4 (1967), 327–51, esp. 328–29. Alemán was not refused permis-
sion to emigrate to Peru in 1582 because he was unable to prove purity of
blood (McGrady, p. 18, mistakenly has Mexico; most recently Bjornson, p.
45) or for any other reason: Cros publishes the official approval, *Bulletin
Hispanique* (above), p. 332. But Alemán chose not to sail. In view of this,
there is no need to explain his large gift to Pedro de Ledesma as a bribe "in
order to overcome the ban against the emigration of New Christians" when
he reapplied in 1607 (McGrady, p. 35; Bjorson, p. 45). He had reason to
show such gratitude, for being allowed to pass off his mistress as his
daughter on the embarcation list (there were strict rules about who could
accompany an emigrant), and possibly for help in his risky business career.
The invention of a spurious and grandiose coat of arms proves nothing
(Marín's final note to his "Documentos"; McGrady, p. 169 n.7). Lope de
Vega did the same. The supposition that Guzmán's ancestry was Jewish is
not supported by the text, but to argue the point would extend this note
intolerably.

2. The rhetorical structure is abundantly studied by Edmond Cros, *Protée et le Gueux*.

3. E.g., Carlos Blanco Aguinaga, "Cervantes y la picaresca," pp. 319, 322.

4. Cros, *Protée*, 88–89.

5. Miller, *The Picaresque Novel*, p. 71.

6. Rico, "Introducción," p. xciii, n. 19 bis.

7. McGrady, *Alemán*, p. 22.

8. Cros, *Protée*.

9. Ibid., p. 52.

10. Ibid., pp. 30–31.

11. George Ticknor, *A History of Spanish Literature* (New York, 1849) p. 59.

12. Oldrich Belič, "La novela picaresca como orden artistico," *Universidad de la Habana*, 27, no. 163 (1963) 7–30. Elizabeth Campuzano, "Ciertos aspectos de la novela picaresca," *Hispania*, 32 (1949), 190–98.

13. J. A. van Praag, "Sobre el sentido del G de A," *Estudios dedicados a Menéndez Pidal*, vol. 5 (Madrid, 1954), pp. 283–86.

14. *Literature and the Delinquent*, p. 45.

15. *Itinerario*, p. 85.

16. Molho, "Introducción" p. 86.

17. Sobejano, "Intención y valor . . . ."

18. *Protée*, chaps. 5–6.

19. McGrady, *Alemán*, chap 8.

20. Cros, *Mateo Alemán*, pt. 2.

21. E.g., McGrady, p. 101; Molho, p. 62.

22. *La novela picaresca y el punto de vista*, p. 61, n. 22.

23. Rico, "Introducción," p. cxxii and n. 22.

24. *Knaves and Swindlers: Essays on the Picaresque in Europe*, ed. Christine J. Whitbourn (London: Oxford University Press, 1974), pp. 12, 42.

25. Cros, *Mateo Alemán*, chap. 6.

26. Oakley, "The Problematic Unity of G de A." *Hispanic Studies in Honour of Joseph Manson* (Oxford: Dolphin Book Co., 1972). p. 206.

27. *Agudeza y arte de ingenio (Ingenuity and Art of Wit)*, discurso 56.

28. McGrady, p. 156. See also the same author's "Consideraciones sobre Ozmín y Daraja de Mateo Alemán," *Revista de Filología Española*, 48 (1965), 281–293.

Chapter Four

1. There is no complete modern biography of Quevedo. James O. Crosby has published numerous documents in the last twenty years in various journals. Still readable and basically sound, by an author who has a sympathetic understanding of Q's aristocratic world is Duque [Miguel] de Maura, *Conferencias sobre Quevedo* (Madrid, [1946?]).

2. F. Lázaro Carreter, "Originalidad del Buscón," in *Studia Philologica. Homenaje a Dámaso Alonso*, vol. 2 (Madrid, 1961), pp. 319–38. See particularly, pp. 324–26.

3. P. N. Dunn, "El individuo y la sociedad en *La vida del Buscón*," *Bulletin Hispanique*, 52 (1950), 375–96; see esp. pp. 385–86 (I no longer subscribe to the moralistic interpretation in the rest of this article); C. B. Morris, *The Unity and Structure of Q's Buscón: Desgracias encadenadas* (Hull: University of Hull Press, 1965) p. 6.

4. E.g., on pages 238–41. Cf. Rico, "Introducción," p. lxvi.

5. May, "Good and Evil in the Buscón: A Survey," *Modern Language Review*, 45 (1950), 319–35.

6. Lázaro, *Originalidad*, p. 327.

7. Ibid, pp. 330, 333.

8. Luis F. de Peñalosa, "Juan Bravo y la familia Coronel," *Estudios segovianos*, 1 (1949), 73–109.

9. Carrol B. Johnson, "*El Buscón:* D. Pablos, D. Diego y D. Francisco," *Hispanófila*, no. 51 (May, 1974), 1–26.

10. *La novela picaresca y el punto de vista*, p. 120.

11. Raimundo Lida, "Pablos de Segovia y su agudeza," in *Homenaje a Joaquín Casalduero* (Madrid: Gredos, 1972), pp. 285–98; see esp. p. 298.

Chapter Five

1. *The Picaresque*, p. 25

2. The matter is dealt with in different, and not always reconcilable, ways by Pamela Waley, "The Unity of the *Casamiento engañoso* and the *Coloquio de los perros*," *Bulletin of Hispanic Studies*, 34 (1956), 201–12; Juan Bautista Avalle-Arce, introduction to *Three Exemplary Novels* (New York: Dell, 1964); Ruth El Saffar, *Cervantes' "El casamineto engañoso" and "El coloquio de los perros,"* (Critical Guides to Spanish Texts [London: Grant & Cutler, 1976]).

3. Cynic, derived from the Greek and meaning "dog." See E.C. Riley, "Cervantes and the Cynics," *Bulletin of Hispanic Studies*, 53 (1976), 189–99, for the latest discussion of the implications of this.

4. Peter N. Dunn, "Las novelas ejemplares," in *Suma Cervantina*, ed. J. B. Avalle-Arce and E. C. Riley (London: Tamesis, 1973), 81–118; see esp. p. 115.

5. Molho, *Introducción al pensamiento picaresco*, p. 126.

6. See, for example, Carlos Blanco Aguinaga, "Cervantes y la picaresca . . . "; Gonzalo Sobejano, "El *Coloquio de los perros* en la picaresca y otros apuntes," *Hispanic Review*, 43 (1975), 25–41.

Chapter Six

1. George Haley, *Vicente Espinel and Marcos de Obregón* (Providence: Brown University Press, 1959).

2. Richard Bjornson, *The Picaresque Hero*, pp. 80–81.

3. Most notably by Gonzalo de Céspedes y Meneses in his *Historias peregrinas y exemplares, con el origen, fundamentos y excelencias de España, y ciudades adonde sucedieron* (Zaragoza, 1623).

4. "Jerónimo de Alcalá y la tradición novelesca," *Estudios segovianos*, 1 (1949), 259–62.

5. The little that is known about Castillo is presented by E. Cotarelo y Mori in the prefaces to *Colección Selecta de Antiguas Novelas Españolas* (Madrid, vol. 3, 1906; vol. 7, 1907), and by F. Ruiz Morcuende in his edition of *La Garduña de Sevilla* (Madrid: Espasa Calpe, 1942). A summary is in Peter N. Dunn, *Castillo Solórzano and the Decline of the Spanish Novel* (Oxford : Blackwell, 1952), pp. vii–viii.

6. The *Tardes entretenidas* were reprinted in *Colección Selecta. . .*, vol. 9 (see n. 5 above).

7. Dunn, *Castillo Solórzano*.

8. See below, chapter 8.

9. Marcel Bataillon has presented the problem, and an intriguing approach to a solution, in "Estebanillo González, bouffon pour rire," in *Studies in Spanish Literature of the Golden Age Presented to Edward M. Wilson*, ed. R. O. Jones (London: Tamesis Books, 1973), pp. 25–44.

10. "Prólogo" to ed. of *La Vida y hechos de Estebanillo González* by Antonio Carreira and Jesús A. Cid, (Madrid: Narcea, 1971). This is a reprint slightly altered, of the article "Estebanillo González, hombre de buen humor," in *Ruedo Ibérico* no. 8 (Aug.–Sept. 1966), 78–86. It is also included in Goytisolo's collection of essays *El furgón de cola* (Paris, 1967).

11. A. A. Parker, *Literature and the Delinquent*, pp. 76–77.

12. Del Monte, *Itinerario*, p. 152.

Chapter Seven

1. *Literature and the Delinquent*, p. 46.

2. Bjornson, *Picaresque Hero*, p. 87.

3. Marcel Bataillon, *Pícaros y picaresca* (Madrid: Taurus, 1969), pp. 180–81.

4. Miguel de Cervantes, *Novelas ejemplares*, 2 vols., ed. F. Rodríguez Marín (Madrid: La Lectura, 1914–17; many reprints by Espasa-Calpe), II, 221–22.

5. *Guzmán de Alfarache*, I, iii, 2.

6. Bataillon, *Pícaros y picaresca*, p. 40.

7. Edwin B. Place, *Manual elemental de novelística española*. Biblioteca española de divulgación científica, vol. 7 (Madrid: Victoriano Suárez, 1926), p. 120.

8. Thomas Hanrahan, S.J., *La mujer en la novela picaresca española*, 2 vols. (Madrid: Porrúa Turanzas, 1967), II, 237–38.

9. *Las Harpías en Madrid*, ed. Cotarelo, p. 4.

10. Alan Francis, *Picaresca, decadencia, historia* (Madrid: Gredos, 1978), p. 143.

Chapter Eight

1. *An Outline of the History of the Novela Picaresca in Spain* (The Hague: Nijhoff, 1903), p. 1.

2. *Romances of Roguery*, p. 43.

3. "Nueva interpretación de la novela picaresca," *Revista de Filología Española*, 24 (1937), 343–62.

4. "Toward a Definition of the Picaresque."

5. "Para una revisión. . . ."

6. In his *Structuralism in Literature* (New Haven: Yale University Press, 1974), pp. 133–41.

7. "The Nature of Picaresque Narrative: A Modal Approach," *PMLA*, 89 (1974), 240–49.

8. Ibid., p. 241a.

9. Joan Rockwell, *Fact in Fiction: The Use of Literature in the Systematic Study of Society* (London: Routledge and Kegan Paul, 1974), p. 104.

10. *Pícaros y Picaresca* (Madrid: Taurus, 1969), pp. 21–27; "Recherches sur les pauvres dans l'ancien Espagne," *Annuaire du Collège de France*, 49 (1949), 209–14.

11. A. Domínguez Ortiz, *The Golden Age of Spain, 1516–1659* (New York: Basic Books, 1971), pp. 174–75.

12. J. H. Elliott, *Imperial Spain, 1469–1716* (London: Arnold, 1963), pp. 292–93; F. Braudel, *The Mediterranean and the Mediterranean World in the Age of Philip II* (New York: Harper, 1973) II, 891–900.

13. Domínguez Ortiz, p. 250.

14. Derek Lomax, "On Re-reading the *Lazarillo de Tormes*," in *Studia Iberica: Festschrift für Hans Flasche* (Bern: Francke, 1973), pp. 371–81.

15. For a start, see H. R. Trevor-Roper, "The General Crisis of the Seventeenth Century," *Past and Present*, no. 16 (November, 1959), 31–64; J. H. Elliot, "The Decline of Spain," *Past and Present*, no. 20 (November, 1961), 52–75; J. H. Elliott, "Self-Perception and Decline in Early Seventeenth-Century Spain," *Past and Present*, no. 74 (February, 1977), 41–61; José Antonio Maravall, *Estado moderno y mentalidad social*, 2 vols. (Madrid: Revista de Occidente, 1972); José Antonio Maravall, *La oposición política bajo los Austrias* (Barcelona; Ariel, 1972); José Antonio Maravall, *La cultura del barroco* (Barcelona: Ariel, 1975); Antonio Domínguez Ortiz, *Crisis y decadencia de la España de los Austrias* (Barcelona: Ariel, 1969); Pierre Vilar; "Le Temps du Quichotte," *Europe* (Paris), 34 (1956).

16. I include his unfortunate assumption that Guzmán represents a converso view of life; cf. above, chapter 3, note 1.

17. Among the numerous writings of Américo Castro on this subject, see especially *De la edad conflictiva*, 2d ed. (Madrid: Taurus, 1963). Also, for a discussion of the possible reflection of the precarious status of conversos in picaros' deviation from respectability, Bataillon, *Picaros y picaresca*, pp. 209–43.

18. Maravall, *La cultura del barroco*.

19. Joseph V. Ricapito, "Société et ambiance historique dans la critique du roman picaresque espagnole," *Actes: Picaresque Espagnole*. Actes de la Table Ronde Internationale du CNRS, Montpellier, Nov. 1974. Études Sociocritiques (Montpellier: Université Paul Valéry, 1976), pp. 9–36.

20. György Lukács, *Die Theorie des Romans* (Berlin, 1920); translated as *The Theory of the Novel* (Cambridge: M.I.T. Press, 1971); *Essays über Realismus (Studies in European Realism* [New York: Grosset, 1964]); Lucien Goldmann, *Pour une sociologie du roman* (Paris: Gallimard, 1965); translated as *Towards a Sociology of the Novel* (London: Tavistock Publications, 1975); Michel Zeraffa, *Roman et société* (Paris: Presses Universitaires de France, 1971).

21. "Le structuralisme génétique en sociologie de la littérature," *Littérature et Société*. Colloque Internationale de Sociologie de la Littérature, 1964 (Brussels: Institut de Sociologie de l'Université Libre de Bruxelles, 1967), pp. 195–211; see p. 204. This essay is translated in *Sociology of Literature and Drama*, ed. Elizabeth and Tom Burns (Harmondsworth: Penguin, 1973), pp. 109–23.

22. Edmond Cros, *L'Aristocrate et le carnaval des gueux, étude sur le "Buscón" de Quevedo* (Montpellier: Centre d'Études Sociocritiques, Université Paul Valéry, 1975); "Approche sociocritique du *Buscón*," in *Actes: Picaresque Espagnole;* "Fundamentos de una sociocrítica: Presupuestos metodológicos y aplicaciones," *Ideologies and Literature*, 1, no. 3 (May–June, 1977), 60–68; "Foundations of a Sociocriticism (Part II). Methodological Proposals and an Application to the Case of the *Buscón*," *Ideologies and Literature*, 1, no. 4, (September–October, 1977), 63–80. Félix Brun, "Pour une interprétation sociologique du roman picaresque," *Littérature et Société* (1967), pp. 127–135; Jean Ignacio Ferreras, "Le problème du sujet collectif en Littérature," *Actes. Picaresque Espagnole*.

23. Peter N. Dunn, "The Spanish Picaresque Novel: Real Societies and Invented Societies," in *Proceedings of the Fiftieth Anniversary Meeting of the F.I.L.L.M.*, Aix-en-Provence, 1978 (forthcoming).

24. Cristóbal de Chaves, *Relación de la cárcel de Sevilla* (written in the 1590s?); Carlos García, *La desordenada codicia de los bienes ajenos* (Paris, 1619). The latter, it has recently been suggested, is a boundary case of picaresque. See M. J. Thacker, "Dr. Carlos García's *La desordenada codicia:*—a *caso límite* of the Picaresque?" *Bulletin of Hispanic Studies*, 55 (1978), 33–41.

25. Edited by A. Bonilla y San Martín in *Revue Hispanique*, 9 (1902), 293–330.

26. Walter L. Reed, "The Problem with a Poetics of the Novel," *Novel*, 9 (1976), 101–113; see p. 103.

27. Interview quoted by Francine du Plessix Gray in *New York Times Book Review*, March 29, 1978, p. 34.

Selected Bibliography

1. Texts

a. Anthologies of complete novels

La novela picaresca española. Vol I. Edited by Francisco Rico. 2d ed. Barcelona: Planeta, 1970. Contains only *Lazarillo de Tormes* and *Guzmán de Alfarache.* Both excellent editions with copious and valuable notes. Fine introduction.

La novela picaresca española. Edited by Joaquín del Val. 3d ed. Madrid: Taurus, 1975. Contains *Lazarillo de Tormes; Guzmán de Alfarache,* Part 1; *Rinconete y Cortadillo; El Buscón.* Reliable.

La novela picaresca española. Edited by Angel Valbuena Prat. 6th ed. Madrid: Aguilar, 1968. Contains all the individual novels studied here, except *Lazarillo de Manzanares* and *El guitón Honofre.* The most extensive anthology available, but not the most scholarly texts. Short on annotation.

b. Individual works (Original edition cited first, followed by most reliable modern version)

ALCALÁ YÁÑEZ, JERÓNIMO DE. *Alonso, mozo de muchos amos.* Part 1. Madrid: Bernardino de Guzmán, 1624. Part 2. Valladolid: Jeronimo Morillo, 1626.

ALEMÁN, MATEO. *Primera parte de Guzmán de Alfarache.* Madrid: Várez de Castro, 1599. *Segunda parte de la vida de Guzmán de Alfarache: Atalaya de la vida humana.* Lisbon: Pedro Crasbeeck, 1604. Edited by Samuel Gili y Gaya (5 vols., Clásicos Castellanos [Madrid: Espasa Calpe, 1926–36]).

CASTILLO SOLÓRZANO, ALONSO DE. *Tardes entretenidas.* Madrid: Viuda de Alonso Martín, 1625.

———. *Las harpías en Madrid y Coche de las estafas.* Barcelona: Sebastián de Cormellas, 1631.

———. *La niña de los embustes, Teresa de Manzanares.* Barcelona: Jerónimo Margarit, 1632. This and the two preceding entries were edited by Emilio Cotarelo y Mori in the *Colección Selecta de Antiguas*

155

Novelas Españolas, vols. 9 (1908), 7 (1907) and 3 (1906) (Madrid: Viuda de Rico). *La niña de los embustes* is also in the anthology by Valbuena Prat.

CASTILLO SOLÓRZANO, ALONSO DE. *Las aventuras del bachiller Trapaza.* Zaragoza: Pedro Vergés, 1637.

———. *La garduña de Sevilla.* Madrid: Imprenta del Reino, 1642. Edited by Federico Ruiz Morcuende (Clásicos Castellanos [Madrid: Espasa Calpe, 1922]).

CERVANTES SAAVEDRA, MIGUEL DE. *Novelas exemplares.* Madrid: Juan de la Cuesta, 1613. Edited by Rodolfo Schevill and Adolfo Bonilla (3 vols. [Madrid: 1925]); and by F. Rodríguez Marín (2 vols., Clásicos Castellanos [Madrid: Espasa Calpe, 1914–17]).

CORTÉS DE TOLOSA, JUAN. *Lazarillo de Manzanares, con otras cinco novelas.* Madrid: Viuda de Alonso Martín, 1620. Edited by Giuseppe E. Sansone (Clasicos Castellanos [Madrid: Espasa-Calpe, 1974]).

ENRÍQUEZ GÓMEZ, ANTONIO. *El siglo pitagórico y vida de don Gregorio Guadaña.* Rouen: Laurent Maurry, 1644. Edited by Charles Amiel (Paris: Ediciones hispano-americanas; Madrid: Castaliá, 1977).

ESPINEL, VICENTE. *Relaciones de la vida del escudero Marcos de Obregón.* Madrid: Juan de la Cuesta, 1618. Edited by Samuel Gili y Gaya (2 vols., Clásicos Castellanos [Madrid: Espasa Calpe, 1951]).

GOMÉZ DE QUEVEDO Y VILLEGAS, FRANCISCO. *La vida del Buscón.* Zaragoza: Roberto Duport, 1626. Edited by F. Lázaro Carreter (Salamanca: C.S.I.C., 1965).

GONZÁLEZ, GREGORIO. *El guitón Honofre* (manuscript). Edited by Hazel G. Carrasco (Chapel Hill, N.C.: Estudios de Hispanófila, 1973).

Vida y hechos de Estebanillo González, hombre de buen humor. Compuesto por el mismo. Antwerp: Viuda de Juan Cnobbart, 1646. Edited by Antonio Carreira and Jesús Antonio Cid (Madrid: Narcea, 1971).

La vida de Lazarillo de Tormes y de sus fortunas y adversidades. [Three separate editions:] Burgos; Antwerp; Alcalá; 1554. Edited by R. O. Jones (Manchester: Manchester University Press, 1963; by Claudio Guillén (with *El Abencerraje*) (New York: Dell, 1966) and by Alberto Blecua (Madrid: Castalia, 1974).

LÓPEZ DE ÚBEDA, FRANCISCO. *Libro de entretenimiento de la Pícara Justina.* Medina del Campo. Edited by Julio Puyol y Alonso (Sociedad de Bibliófilos Madrileños, vols. 7–9 [Madrid, 1912]).

LUJÁN DE SAYAVEDRA, MATEO. [i.e., Juan Martí]. *Segunda parte del pícaro Guzmán de Alfarache.* Valencia? 1602? A recent edition is available in the anthology by Valbuena Prat.

LUNA, JUAN DE. *Segunda parte de Lazarillo de Tormes.* Paris: Rolet Boutonné, 1620. Edited by Martín de Riquer in *La Celestina y Lazarillos* (Barcelona: Vergara, 1959).

SALAS BARBADILLO, ALONSO JERÓNIMO DE. *La hija de Celestina.* Zaragoza: Viuda de Lucas Sánchez, 1612. Expanded version, *La ingeniosa Elena, hija de Celestina* (Madrid: Juan de Herrera, 1614).

2. Translations

a. Individual authors

ALEMAN. *The Rogue, or The Life of Guzmán de Alfarache.* Translated by James Mabbe. London, 1622. This was a best-seller in seventeenth-century England, but is not easy reading today. There is no modern version in English. This edition edited by James Fitzmaurice-Kelly (London: Constable, 1924; reprint New York: AMS Press, 1967).

CASTILLO SOLÓRZANO. *La Picara: Or The Triumphs of Female Subtility* [*La garduña de Sevilla*]. Translated by John Davies of Kidwelly. London: 1665.

————. *The Spanish Pole-Cat.* Translated by Sir Roger L'Estrange and J. Ozell. London, 1717.

CERVANTES. *Exemplarie Novells in Sixe Books.* Translated by "Don Diego Puede-Ser" James Mabbe. London, 1640.

————. *Six Exemplary Novels.* Translated by Harriet de Onís. New York: Barron's, 1961.

ESPINEL. *The History of the Life of the Squire Marcos de Obregón.* Translated by Algernon Langton. London, 1816. Unreliable.

LAZARILLO DE TORMES. *The Pleasaunt Historie of Lazarillo de Tormes.* Translated by David Rowland of Anglesey. London, 1586. Edited by J. E. V. Crofts (Oxford: Blackwell's, 1924).

QUEVEDO. *The Life and Adventures of Buscon the Witty Spaniard.* Translated by "A Person of Honour." London, 1657.

————. *Life of Paul, the Spanish Sharper.* In *Comical Works of Quevedo,* translated by Captain John Stevens. London, 1709. Revised by Pedro Pineda, 1743.

————. *The Life of the Great Rascal.* In *Quevedo: The Choice Humorous and Satirical Works,* translated by Charles Duff. London: Routledge; New York: Dutton, 1926.

b. Collections

The Spanish Libertines. Translated by John Stevens. London, 1707. A digest containing selections from works such as *Estebanillo González* which are otherwise not available in an English version.

Two Spanish Picaresque Novels: Lazarillo de Tormes [and] *The Swindler* [*El Buscón*]. Translated by Michael Alpert. Harmondsworth: Penguin Classics, 1969.

3. Studies

a. Bibliographies

LAURENTI, JOSEPH L. *Bibliografía de la literatura picaresca* [*Bibliography of Picaresque Literature*]. Metuchen, N.J.: Scarecrow Press, 1973. The most complete bibliography to date.

RICAPITO, JOSEPH V. *Bibliografía razonada y anotada de las obras maestras de la novela picaresca española*. Madrid: Castalia, 1976. Good review and summary of critical opinion on the major authors and topics.

b. Books

Actes: Picaresque Espagnole. Actes de la Table Ronde Internationale du CNRS, Montpellier, Nov. 1974. Études Sociocritiques. Montpellier: Université Paul Valéry, 1976. Papers from a symposium on the sociology of the picaresque novel.

ALTER, ROBERT. *Rogue's Progress: Studies in the Picaresque Novel*. Cambridge: Harvard University Press, 1964. Chapter 1 is on *Lazarillo*, and establishing the "picaresque code." The rest treats Lesage, Defoe, Smollett, and later writers.

BATAILLON, MARCEL. *El Sentido del Lazarillo de Tormes*. Paris: Librairie des Éditions Espagnoles, 1954. Corrects earlier critics' stress on direct social satire.

―――. *Novedad y fecundidad del Lazarillo de Tormes*. 2d ed. Salamanca: Anaya, 1973. Fine study of source materials and their integration; also studies continuations of *Lazarillo*.

―――. *Pícaros y picaresca*. Madrid: Taurus, 1969. The first book to make convincing sense of *La Pícara Justina*.

BJORNSON, RICHARD. *The Picaresque Hero in European Fiction*. Madison:University of Wisconsin Press, 1977. Broad study of picaro in society, in Spain, France, Germany, England. Abundant bibliographical information in notes.

CASTRO, AMÉRICO. *Hacia Cervantes*. Rev. ed. Madrid: Taurus, 1967. Collection of essays, some on picaresque and especially on its relation to social tensions.

CHANDLER, FRANK WADLEIGH. *Romances of Roguery*. New York: Macmillan, 1899. The first detailed large-scale study in English. Still readable, with valuable bibliography of early editions and translations.

CROS, EDMOND. *Protée et le gueux: Recherches sur les origines et la nature du récit picaresque dans "Guzmán de Alfarache."* Paris: Didier, 1967. A vast study of the novel's composition in relation to contemporary intellectual problems and rhetorical practice.

―――. *Mateo Alemán: Introducción a su vida y a su obra*. Salamanca: Anaya, 1971. The most up-to-date life of Alemán, based on the author's own documentary research, followed by a valuable analysis of the novel.

————. *L'Aristocrate et le carnaval des gueux: Etude sur le Buscon de Quevedo. Etudes sociocritiques.* Montpellier: Université Paul Valéry, 1975. Study of the "structural homologies" in the text, interprets the novel in terms of the language of carnival burlesque which is the setting for acts of justice and punishment.

DE HAAN, FONGER. *An Outline of the Novela Picaresca in Spain.* The Hague: Nijhoff, 1903. An early attempt to give a consistent model for picaresque. Concise and still readable.

DEL MONTE, ALBERTO. *Itinerario de la novela picaresca.* Barcelona: Editorial Lumen, 1971. Translation of Italian original, *Itinerario del romanzo picaresco spagnolo* (Firenze: Sansoni, 1957). Spanish version is revised to date. Thorough, stresses social background. Copious bibliographical notes.

DEYERMOND, ALAN D. *Lazarillo de Tormes: A Critical Guide.* Critical Guides to Spanish Texts, no. 15. London: Grant and Cutler, 1975. Succinct, remarkably inclusive in a short space. Fine, well-balanced introduction to the novel.

FRANCIS, ALAN. *Picaresca, decadencia, historia: Aproximación a una realidad histórico-literaria.* Madrid: Gredos, 1978. Attempts to examine relation of picaresque novels to Spain's decline in the seventeenth century. See our comments in chapter 8.

GUILLEN, CLAUDIO. *Literature as System.* Princeton: Princeton University Press, 1971. Contains essays previously printed separately. "Toward a Definition of the Picaresque," pp. 71–105, and "Genre and Countergenre: The Discovery of the Picaresque," pp. 136–58, have had great influence on discussions of picaresque as a genre.

HALEY, GEORGE. *Vicente Espinel and Marcos de Obregón: A Life and Its Literary Representation.* Providence: Brown University Press, 1959. The only complete life of Espinel in English. Shows the blending of fact and fiction in *Marcos de Obregón.*

HANRAHAN, THOMAS, S. J. *La mujer en la novela picaresca española.* 2 vols. Madrid: Porrua Turanzas, 1967. Sees the negative role of women in picaresque fiction as consequence of the didactic function of the novels.

LAZARO CARRETER, FERNANDO. *Lazarillo de Tormes en la Picaresca.* Barcelona: Ariel, 1972. Brings together three earlier essays on the fusion of folk-tale elements in *Lazarillo,* and the constitution of the picaresque form. Outstanding example of formalist criticism.

MCGRADY, DONALD. *Mateo Alemán.* New York: Twayne, 1968. The only general introduction to Alemán in English.

MILLER, STUART. *The Picaresque Novel.* Cleveland: Case Western Reserve University Press, 1967. Attempts to isolate typical motifs of picaresque and to study their combination in particular works. Deals with a limited number of Spanish and English novels.

MOLHO, MAURICE. *Introducción al pensamiento picaresco.* Salamanca: Anaya, 1972. Translation of the long introduction to the author's anthology of picaresque novels in French: *Romans Picaresques Espagnols* (Paris: Gallimard, 1968). Essentially a long essay on *Lazarillo, Guzmán,* and *El Buscón,* focussing on the social uneasiness they express. One of the best surveys.

MORENO BAEZ, ENRIQUE. *Lección y sentido del "Guzmán de Alfarache."* Madrid: C.S.I.C., 1948. Exhaustive analysis of the doctrinal Christian themes of the novel.

PARKER, ALEXANDER A. *Literature and the Delinquent: The Picaresque Novel in Spain and Europe, 1599–1753.* Edinburgh: Edinburgh University Press, 1967. Spanish translation: *Los pícaros en la literatura (La novela picaresca en España y Europa: 1599–1753).* (Madrid: Gredos, 1971). This is the most energetic argument for the purely thematic description of picaresque: delinquency as a way of representing the moral problems of freedom.

RICO, FRANCISCO. *La novela picaresca y el punto de vista.* Barcelona: Seix Barral, 1970. A study of narrative point of view in the picaresque novel. Vigorous and contentious. Rico and Lázaro Carreter have effectively brought picaresque into a postformalist era of criticism.

SAN MIGUEL, ANGEL. *Sentido y estructura del "Guzman de Alfarache" de Mateo Alemán.* Madrid: Gredos, 1971. A clear and systematic analysis of the themes in the novel and their development.

SIEBER, HARRY. *Language and Society in La Vida de Lazarillo de Tormes.* Baltimore: The Johns Hopkins Univ. Press, 1978. In the light of Lazarillo's claim to honor as a writer, Sieber explores the many functions of language in the novel, particularly Lazarillo's acquisition and mastery of the linguistic techniques by which he creates himself as hero of his narrative. A "semiotic" account which is both original and readable.

————. *The Picaresque.* The Critical Idiom, no. 33. London: Methuen, 1977. Brief but balanced and well-informed survey of Spanish and European picaresque fiction.

ZAMORA VICENTE, ALONSO. *¿Qué es la novela picaresca?* Buenos Aires: Columbia, 1962. An elementary unpretentious survey for the uninitiated.

C. Articles

BATAILLON, MARCEL. "Estebanillo Gonzalez, bouffon pour rire." In *Studies in Spanish Literature of the Golden Age Presented to Edward M. Wilson;* edited by R. O. Jones, pp. 25–44. London: Tamesis Books,

1973. An original approach to the problem of authorship of the *Life* of Estebanillo, and the status of the narrator.

BLANCO AGUINAGA, CARLOS. "Cervantes y la picaresca: Notas sobre dos tipos de realismo." *Nueva Revista de Filología Hispánica*, 11 (1957), 314–42. English translation: "Cervantes and the Picaresque Mode: Notes on Two Kinds of Realism," in Lowry J. Nelson, ed. *Cervantes: A Collection of Critical Essays, Twentieth Century Views* (Englewood Cliffs: Prentice Hall, 1969), pp. 137–51 (somewhat abridged). Argues that Cervantes' aesthetics are totally opposed to picaresque.

GUILLEN, CLAUDIO. "La disposición temporal del *Lazarillo de Tormes*." *Hispanic Review*, 25 (1957), 264–79. A classic essay, on the creation of the sense of experienced time in *Lazarillo*.

LAZARO CARRETER, FERNANDO. "Originalidad del *Buscón*." In *Studia Philologica: Homenaje a Dámaso Alonso*, vol. 2. Madrid: Gredos, 1961. Pp. 319–38. A vigorous assertion that *El Buscón* is a display of wit and ruthless caricature, without moral or social intention.

LIDA, RAIMUNDO. "Pablos de Segovia y su agudeza: Notas sobre la lengua del *Buscón*." In *Homenaje a Casalduero*. Madrid: Gredos, 1972, pp. 285–98.

―――. "Sobre el arte verbal del *Buscón*." *Philological Quarterly*, 51, (1972), 255–69. These two papers are an excellent analysis of Quevedo's wordplay.

MARAVALL, JOSE ANTONIO. "La aspiración social de 'medro' en la novela picaresca." *Cuadernos hispanoamericanos*, no. 312 (June, 1976), 590–625. Relates the picaro's desire to "get ahead," to marginality, as perceived in the seventeenth century.

MAY, TERENCE E. "Good and Evil in the Buscón: A Survey." *Modern Language Review*, 45 (1950), 319–35. Sees religious symbols (Pablos refusing his cross) which are read as confirming the picaro's flight into unreality.

PARKER, ALEXANDER A. "The Psychology of the Picaro in *El Buscón*." *Modern Language Review*, 42 (1947), 58–69. Interprets Pablos' career as an example of the psychology of compensation.

SCOBIE, ALEXANDER. *Aspects of the Ancient Romance and Its Heritage*. Beiträge zur Klassischen Philolgie, no. 30. Meisenheim a Glan: Hain, 1969. Considers the possible influence of Latin literature, Apuleius and Petronius in particular, on the formation of the Spanish picaresque novel.

SERRANO PONCELA, SEGUNDO. "¿*El Buscón*—Parodia picaresca?" *Insula*, 12, no. 154 (1959), 1, 10. Reprinted in *Del Romancero a Machado* (Caracas: Facultad de Letras, 1962), pp. 87–101. One of the first to suggest that Quevedo was parodying the earlier picaresque novels.

SPITZER, LEO. "Zur Kunst Quevedos in seinem *Buscón*," *Archivum Romanicum*, 11 (1927), 511–80. French translation: *L'art de Quevedo dans le Buscón* (Paris: Ediciones hispano-americanas: Travaux de l'Institut d'Etudes Ibéro et Latinoaméricains de l'Université de Strasbourg, 1972). Spitzer saw the novel as a vehicle of picaresque "disillusion," but the novel itself fails to integrate its tensions.

TARR, F. COURTNEY. "Literary and Artistic Unity in the *Lazarillo de Tormes*." *PMLA*, 42 (1927), 404–44. The first account of *Lazarillo* as a coherent whole, this study is still valuable.

WARDROPPER, BRUCE W. "El trastorno de la moral en el *Lazarillo*." *Nueva Revista de Filogía Hispanica*, 15 (1961), 441–47. Lazarillo reveals the "seamy side" of his existence, as he tries to conceal it.

WICKS, ULRICH. "The Nature of Picaresque Narrative: A Modal Approach." *PMLA*, 89 (1974), 240–49. Following Robert Scholes, proposes "'mode" as a way of avoiding the form/theme problems in defining picaresque.

Index